the DIVISION of HEAVEN and EARTH

the DIVISION of HEAVEN and EARTH

ON TIBET'S PEACEFUL REVOLUTION

SHOKDUNG

Translated by MATTHEW AKESTER

SPEAKING TIGER

SPEAKING TIGER PUBLISHING PVT. LTD
4381/4, Ansari Road, Daryaganj,
New Delhi–110002, India

First published by C. Hurst & Co. (Publishers) Ltd., 2016
First published in India by Speaking Tiger in hardback 2017

ISBN: 978-93-86582-13-3
eISBN: 978-93-86582-14-0

10 9 8 7 6 5 4 3 2 1

Printed at Gopsons Papers Ltd

CONTENTS

INTRODUCTION

Sonam Tsering

Translated by
Matthew Akester

The Division of Heaven and Earth celebrates the courage of the people who took part in the peaceful uprising of 2008 in Tibet and looks at future possibilities for peaceful protest, introducing some of the basic ideas behind it. The Chinese government banned the book as soon as it was published and arrested the author. At that time, Shokdung was known as an opponent of religion in Tibetan society rather than as an opponent of the politics of the Chinese state, but now that he has antagonised both the Chinese state and Tibetan society in different ways, this book can be seen as a milestone marking his move into political opposition.

Like other colonising imperialists, the People's Republic of China has sought to control not only the territory of Tibet but the minds of Tibetans as well, since 1951. To gain control over Tibetan minds, the Chinese government established a mass media including newspapers, radio and television and used modern technology to propagate Marxist ideology in Tibetan society and in the Tibetan language. To strengthen and ensure the continuity of the propaganda effort, they set up schools in each locality where it was taught that the old Tibetan society was backward and dark and Tibetan students should look to the Chinese Communist Party for help in developing their society. They still teach this to all students from primary school level up to university. The government sees this as one of its contests with the Dalai Lama: to gain a fundamental influence over Tibetan society.

The author of this book, Tragya, (pen name, Shokdung), is a Tibetan man who grew up under the Chinese government's education system. On 2 May 1999, to mark the anniversary of the 4 May 1919 student movement, Tragya published an article in the state newspaper, *Qinghai Tibetan News*, under the pen name Shokdung, headlined 'Blood-letting to kill the tumour of ignorance'. In it, he took the Marxist view that 'the new cannot be established without destroying the old', arguing that Tibetan society and culture were backward, and for them to develop, the engrained influence of Buddhism on Tibetan attitudes must be wiped out. The article, written independently of his job in a government publishing house, provoked fierce debate as soon as it was circulated in Tibetan society, and institutions such as the Qinghai People's Radio and Qinghai Nationalities University organised meetings for Shokdung to explain his ideas directly to the public.

Although not welcomed by the clergy or the public, Shokdung continued to write articles and give talks through various channels, official and unofficial, on the need to revolutionise traditional Tibetan culture founded on Buddhism. A collection of these was also published as a book.

He saw himself as sounding the call of the morning conch shell trumpet, awakening Tibetan society from the ignorance of backwardness. His pen name, Shokdung, is derived from this idea.

INTRODUCTION

The idea that Tibet cannot progress without transforming its Buddhist culture is not unique to Shokdung. It is a founding principle of the government's modern Tibetan literature. The international Tibetology community questions whether modern Tibetan literature is literature or propaganda.

Pema Bhum, who once taught modern literature at the Northwest Minorities University where Shokdung studied, described the outlook of intellectuals at the time. He said that they faced a choice between two systems of thought upon which to base their thinking and in which to believe. The first, Marxism-Leninism, came to Tibet with a hostile army, and is associated by all Tibetans with the multitude of troubles and hardships it created there. The second is Buddhism, which the Tibetan people have revered and supported for a thousand years, yet it did not protect them. Seeing this, these intellectuals, despairing of both doctrines, believed there was no one else to rely upon except themselves.

Their poetry was a revolutionary struggle for freedom within the realm of ideas.

These Tibetan intellectuals saw great value in humanism and modernism from the ideas of the European Enlightenment, and from that perspective they interpreted Tibetan history in ways that challenged the hegemonic sense of tradition based on religious orthodoxy.

With this kind of approach, Shokdung claimed that for a thousand years since the fall of the Tibetan empire, the Tibetan people had been taken in by the 'Non-self' doctrine of Buddhism, and had thus lost the 'Self' of imperial territoriality and ancestry. Therefore, unless the engrained influences of the Buddhist 'Non-self' on the Tibetan psyche were erased, they would never realise the 'Self' of imperial territoriality and ancestry.

As they struggled for intellectual freedom, Tibetan intellectuals experienced many ideological contradictions. Whether the formation of their mentality can be attributed solely to the Chinese education system is hard to say, but they harbour an uncompromising and abiding concern for Tibet, one that belongs neither to the church nor the Communist Party.

Unlike other contemporary Tibetan writers, Shokdung has chosen a naked form of expression, eschewing poetry and literary technique, to express his view of the need to revolutionise traditional culture. The articles that appeared in the official Party newspaper (there was a second in July 1999) offended traditionalists quite badly, and from 2 May 1999 to 1 June 2000, the *Qinghai Tibetan News* office received over 40 articles and letters to the editor, as well as two telephone death threats against Shokdung.

At that time, many in Tibetan society called Shokdung a 'heretic', 'red guard', 'anti-religionist', 'tool of the Chinese government' and so on. Dondrup Gyal, often regarded as the father of modern Tibetan literature, wrote in the 1980s in response to such attitudes: 'I myself may become a target for praise or blame, but I am determined to oppose them [the traditional intellectual class] as long as I live.' There have been divisions between modern intellectuals who have been through the Chinese state education system and traditional intellectuals in the monasteries over attitudes towards Buddhism and traditional learning, but such divisions are liable to diminish rather than grow, as can be seen from the present work.

The Division of Heaven and Earth was written after witnessing the wave of protests that swept throughout Tibet in 2008, especially among the Tibetan inhabitants of the Chinese frontier, the supposed descendants of Tibet's imperial army, who decked their horses with snow lion flags, and shouted war cries of 'Kiki Soso!'. They rode up to the local Chinese government offices, pulled down the red national flags and replaced them with the [Tibetan] snow lion flag. Written to celebrate the courage of their protest, the book also considers suitable methods for non-violent protest in the future, and introduces Tibetan readers to the philosophy of non-violent activism.

Unlike his earlier writings on revolutionising old thinking, this book is about political freedom and the struggle to attain it. Earlier, Shokdung had generally ignored politics and freedom in the collective sense, and written only of the freedom of inner thoughts and ideas. This made people angry, and he had plenty of detractors, but he does not accept the criticism, seeing the growth of awareness of freedom, equality and rights in our inner thoughts as an essential preparation. He sees the events of 2008 as showing that Tibetans have now taken up the struggle for freedom and rights in practice as well as in thought, prompting him to write about the methods of struggle for collective or civil freedoms.

The book is written in two parts. The first describes the author's experience of three strong emotions: joy, sorrow and fear, sparked by the 2008 protests.

The chapter on joy proposes that while the causes of the protests were of course related to political repression, economic exploitation and cultural changes, even more importantly, it was through the rigours of these experiences that the sense of national identity, a vestige of imperial times, re-awakened from within—that is the courage to seek the 'Self' of imperial territoriality and ancestry. The Tibetan people, who had even lost control of their own country because of devoting so much attention to religion in the past, have at the start of the 21st century, finally begun to develop awareness of their territory and their rights, and to seek freedom and equality, the preparation for self-reliance, which is cause for joy. Whatever is broadcast about Tibet in the course of this struggle, true or false, brings publicity and attention to the Tibetan issue, serves to generate awareness, and strengthens the impression that China's treatment of Tibet needs to change, demonstrating to the younger generation the purpose and direction of future struggles.

In the section on sorrow, Shokdung recalls how having gained some degree of political awareness and launched a peaceful struggle for freedom and equality, the Chinese government branded this as 'beating, smashing, looting and burning' and responded with violent repression. He suggests that this misery is the Karmic result of Tibetans having lived in a religious dream world up to now. The responsibility for this lies with religion, the Lamas and Tulkus, which is why, he says, 'I stir them, shake them up, raise doubts, argue with them or refute them'. However, seeing signs that the Tibetan people are starting to wake up means that it is time for us to gain familiarity with many secular matters of which the previous generation preferred to remain ignorant, and he offers a convenient list of the features of a totalitarian political system informed by Tibetan experience, and based on the definition by Chinese scholar Hu Xi.

Discussing fear, he writes of how the government not only branded the peaceful protests as 'beating, smashing, looting and burning', but used the weapons left in Tibetan protector chapels as ornaments of the deity as an excuse to try and label the movement as a 'terrorist' campaign. Moreover, to shore up and prevent threats to its power, the government encouraged a wave of nationalism among the Chinese population, producing extreme nationalist sentiments such as 'Kill all the Tibetans! Wipe them out!'

Tibetans lack experience in political struggle, and there were indeed incidents of 'beating, smashing, looting and burning' in some places, but they were due to nothing more than over-excitement and copycat behaviour. Nonetheless, it is not impossible that out of desperation, Tibetans will resort to violence, assassination and killing for example, and while compassion is supposed to be the dominant moral value, there is also the extremist religious view that those who are obliged to kill in defence of the Buddhist teachings will not go to hell. Seeing that such an eventuality would be to hand the Chinese government all the pretexts it needs to crack down on protest and risk losing international support for the Tibetan cause, Shokdung argues that Tibet's peaceful protest movement needs a method of action, a founding principle and basis, and that is non-violent non-cooperation, or the 'Truth Insistence' of Gandhi, which is described in the second part of the book.

He states that introducing methods of peaceful protest is the main purpose of this book and he begins by introducing the right to civil disobedience and its establishment as a form of political action since the time of Henry David Thoreau. To show how individuals can practise civil disobedience, he gives the example of Socrates' death in ancient Greece, as related by Plato in the Crito chapter of the 'Dialogues'. He further mentions examples of the theory and practice of civil disobedience from the Christian New Testament and other Western religious and philosophical treatises, spanning the ages, and presenting the subject to a Tibetan audience in terms easy to understand and retain. The author's objective in this is only to give Tibetans counsel on how people in Europe and North America used non-retaliation to deny the government a pretext to crack down on protests and used non-violent means to show the legitimacy of their protest, but he makes it clear that the value of civil disobedience pertains only to democratic societies, and does not figure in authoritarian societies.

The second part of this section is an introduction to the non-violent methods of Gandhi's Satyagraha or 'Truth Insistence'. Shokdung explains how these methods freed India from nearly two centuries of British colonialism without the loss of many Indian lives. He shows in some detail that Satyagraha is not just a means of political action, but part of a religious and moral philosophy, by discussing the origins of Gandhi's thought and its conception of the value of human life. His hope is that Tibetans, especially the Lamas and Tulkus, will see in Satyagraha the most suitable means for pursuing the Tibetan struggle. He also adds a presentation on universal values and the Universal Declaration of Human Rights as appendices, to help Tibetan readers become more familiar with these concepts.

In this section, Shokdung notes that 'Within Tibet, it is the case (at least in Amdo) that the truisms uttered by one simple-minded Lama have more currency than the counsels of a hundred wise laymen', and his own counsels are 'of no more use than the written word is to a musician', so on reflection 'the writing of this book is just a way to relieve the agonies of conscience', showing as it does the alienation and desperation in Tibetan society, or at least a part of it. However, in his discussion of Gandhi's Satyagraha, he does provide readers with a fresh perspective when he says that although the political environment in India under British rule is quite different from Tibet under Chinese rule, we must also consider the similar influence of religious culture in both countries.

In terms of strategy, he sees a new value for the role of religious influence. Religion and the traditional culture that he has consistently criticised in the past can be valuable assets in the political struggle against Chinese colonialism. He welcomes the use of religious forms such as boycotting New Year celebrations, staging candle-lit marches, fasting and so on to protest against the Chinese government and views them as effective non-violent non-cooperation, and concludes the closing chapter of the book with the hope that Tibetans can conduct a peaceful protest movement 'with Khata scarves, rosaries or butter lamps in hand'.

In summary, in *The Division of Heaven and Earth* we see how a Tibetan raised in an education system based on Marxist values, who has publicly called for the destruction of religion and traditional culture in a Communist Party newspaper, appraises the 2008 protests. Now Tibetans with a formal education no longer regard religion and traditional values as obstacles on the path for the struggle for freedom and happiness, but rather they are starting to see them as a powerful force in that struggle. We see that Tibetan peoples' thinking is not to be understood in terms of a division between the extremes of modernity and tradition, backwardness and progress, but rather of the mutual accommodation, combination and contradiction between these extremes. In modern Tibetan studies, there is much discussion about Tibetan identity in modern literature, painting, music and so on, but this book reminds us that the debate must look beyond the impact only of European ideas like Marxism-Leninism to which Tibetans have been exposed by the Chinese education system, and move beyond the static opposition of traditionalism and modernism, East and West.

Sonam Tsering was born in Rebgong, Amdo and later lived in the Tibetan community in exile in India. He graduated from the School of Oriental and African Studies, University of London, in 2005 and currently he teaches Tibetan language and culture at Columbia University, New York.

FOREWORD

Françoise Robin, Paris

Shokdung first gained celebrity among Westerners, and more precisely Tibet specialists, through the American Tibetologist Lauran Hartley's careful study of the controversy that he had raised in the late 1990s and early 2000.[1] While she was spending one year in Xining (capital of Qinghai province, where Shokdung lives and works, like a number of Amdo Tibetan intellectuals), Hartley was able to follow day by day the heated discussions that were triggered by Shokdung's iconoclastic essay 'Blood-Letting that will Overcome the Tumor of Ignorance: Against the Old Decaying Propensities', in which he called for a critical re-evaluation of the impact of Tibetan Buddhism on ordinary Tibetans' sense of self and identity and, ultimately, 'modernity'. As is well known, Tibet was and still is characterized by a heavily religious cultural environment. Buddhism and, to a lesser extent, Bon, reincarnated lamas and clergy, as well as monasteries, were and are often considered the key pillars of Tibetan society and the backbone of a Tibetan sense of identity. This is especially true in the critical situation that Tibet has been going through for the last few decades. It is thus easily understandable that Shokdung's blunt criticism of tradition and religiosity met with controversy.

Many Tibetans at that time, mainly from Amdo where Shokdung comes from, took sides: either Shokdung had fallen prey to the Chinese state propaganda on Tibet's alleged 'backwardness' attributed to excessive religiosity and power of the clergy, and he was a traitor to a Tibetan civilisation already in jeopardy; or he was a savior who was at long last coming to grips with the vexed question of Tibetan modernity, by offering what Dan Smyer Yu has called an 'anti-traditionalist imagining of a modern Tibet', which Yu analyses as a subaltern power discourse.[2] A portion of educated lay youngsters approved of his radicalism, while a substantial fraction of the clergy was against him. Even though the masses for the most part did not read his texts—illiteracy is still high in Tibet and his ideas are not always simple to grasp, partly because he suggest many neologisms to express new concepts—they did hear about him and of the controversy. In all events, many Tibetans agreed on one point: whether he was right or wrong, Shokdung mattered because he had made Tibetans think and debate. In a society where public debate about fundamental social choices and models of society had been confiscated by the ruling Communist Party of China (CPC), this was no small feat.

After the shockwaves he made in the early 2000s, Shokdung published three more books, all bearing his trademark:[3] in these he appealed to Tibetan people to develop a sense of scepticism on proclaimed truths, to train one's critical mind and individual thinking, so to build an identity or self, which he hoped would lead to the emergence of what he thought was the modern individual Tibetan, which for him was still missing. Once again, he denounced the ascendancy of Tibetan Buddhism and its focus on non-self and emptiness. According to his contested—and, to some, shallow—views about religion, such core concepts pertaining to *Mahayana* Buddhism have acted as an obstacle towards the emergence of the consciousness of an individual, as well as of freedom, science and modernity. Under the influence of Tibetan Buddhism, and that of *tulkus*[4] 'professing the meaninglessness of cyclic existence', he claimed, ordinary Tibetans have not been able to develop a sense of self or oneself as an individual. As a consequence, ideas resulting from individualism such as democracy, individual rights, freedom, and equality, could not take firm ground in the collective or individual Tibetan mind. In the final analysis, Tibetans' sorry fate under current circumstances was not to be blamed on 'others', which has become a code-name for 'Han Chinese' in Tibet today, but on Tibetans themselves, and more precisely the core component of its culture, i.e. Buddhism, which had hampered their capacity to develop the conceptual and political tools necessary to defend themselves and acquire political modernity. Needless to say, his writings were not welcomed by all strata of Tibetan society. Although they did not lead to the same heated discussions as in 1999–2000, it was reported that they were contested by the charismatic cleric Khenpo Tshultrim Lodro, spiritual heir to the famous lama Khenpo Jigme Phuntso (1937–2004), an advocate and proponent of Buddhist modernism *à la tibétaine*.[5]

Shokdung's name gained renewed currency in 2009, when he published this book, *Division of Sky and Earth*, which was printed without a formal authorization from the official publishing authorities, a rather common fate for potentially 'troublesome' books. As I was not in Tibet at that time, I was unable to assess its impact on the ground, but it quickly became news outside Tibet. Tibetan exile websites launched discussions about the book in the Tibetan language. These discussions soon turned into unanimous praise. As the book reached the West in PDF format, I could cast a first glance at it. It was a shock: it reassessed, from a Tibetan point of view within Tibet, the 2008 'Tibetan uprising' and called for civil disobedience. It claimed that, at long last, after centuries of being astray, Tibetans from all walks of life had started 'to develop a consciousness of their statehood, sovereignty, political, territorial, national and human identity, awareness of freedom, equality, rights, selfhood and democracy, and opposition to autocratic domination.' Shokdung saw the 2008 uprising as an indication that his wish for an awakening of the Tibetan self had been fulfilled, proving his previous views wrong, which he admitted in the introduction to the present book. Shokdung's public praise and assessment of the 2008 movement was a bold move on the part of any Tibetan and, more particularly, on the part of someone who was employed by the state-run Qinghai Nationality Publishing House.

The book, with an initial print run of 1,000 copies, circulated unhindered in Xining and all over Tibet for six months, until the author was arrested on 23 April 2010, an arrest he had foreseen and contemplated with anguish in his book: 'I may lose my head because of my mouth.' It was known later that he had written in anticipation of his arrest a letter to his employer to explain the content of his book and his reasons for writing it, in the likely case he might be arrested. But it was initially argued among Western Tibet specialists that his arrest was due to the appeal he and his long-time intellectual friends had made, three days after the Jyekundo (Chinese: Yushu) earthquake (14 April 2010), which devastated a whole region populated with Tibetans. Jyekundo lies in Qinghai province but is mostly populated by Kham Tibetans. Shokdung and his friends had called for Tibetans not to donate money to the Qinghai Red Cross, openly expressing their suspicion that some of the donations might be embezzled by unscrupulous agents of this state-related relief agency. They argued it was preferable to donate money to private, low-profile, small-scale, Tibetan-run organizations, and they immediately set up their own relief team. Although this call to caution towards a state-run agency was certainly not welcomed by the Chinese authorities, especially as it hailed from a group of influential Tibetans, it was not the main reason for arresting him, he privately said later. Most of his friends who had made the same appeal were not arrested. The reason why he was arrested, according to Shokdung himself, was the present book. If this text displeased the authorities so much, I asked him in 2011, why did it take six months before they banned it and arrested its author? Why did they run the risk to let it circulate unhindered? According to Shokdung again, when news about the book reached them, the authorities decided to have it translated into Chinese to check its content, but also to have it carefully read in its original Tibetan version by four to five persons, with a view to assessing whether *The Division* represented any breach of law. Until now, of course, Shokdung does not know who these evaluators were. He mentioned that they might have taken their time deliberately to read it, enabling the book to circulate freely before its interdiction, a typical trick exercised by reluctant censors. In any case, half a year after the book was published, its content was considered illegal, Shokdung was arrested, and all copies of his books in circulation were confiscated. Shokdung's bookshop, 1+1, which of course kept copies, was closed down too, thus depriving his family of a source of income.

By the time I arrived in Amdo in summer 2010, *The Division* had thus been banned for four months. Still, many educated people, most of them young (Shokdung is popular among college students), kept a copy, hidden in their cupboards under a stack of clothes or at the back of a drawer. At least four different illegal editions were circulating, I was told. Readers were eager to talk discreetly about the banned book, and praised Shokdung's boldness, while lamenting his disappearance. Still, older and more conservative representatives of the educated Tibetan elite were inflamed by what they interpreted as the anti-Buddhist views he had expressed in some of his previous works, and suspected him of having tried, through the book translated here, to reconcile himself with a substantial fraction of the Tibetan population which he had antagonised by his radicalism. At that time, he had been held incommunicado for four months, no one knew with certainty how he was being treated, what was in store for him, whether he was being tortured, what accusations might be made against him, and so forth. His family worried especially because they were not allowed to hand him the medicines he needed to take. His family and co-villagers would often come to the Xining detention center where they thought he was being held, to demonstrate and ask for his release, but they were never allowed to meet him—they did not even know whether he was actually kept there. In spite of doubts and anguish, everyone was adamant that he would not yield to pressure and that he would never renounce his views. This added to the awe and respect that he generated, regardless of what most people had until then thought about him and his radical ideas. From now onwards, Shokdung was the first person who had thoroughly assessed the 2008 Tibet spring revolt by challenging each and every position of the Chinese official media in the form of a full-length book. For instance, he had dared to call the uprising a 'peaceful revolution', a clear contestation of the mainstream Chinese media that kept calling it (and still does) the '3.14 incident', a labeling tending to reduce a month-long, large-scale, popular Tibetan movement to a one-day instance of unjustified violence inflicted by savage Tibetans to harmless Chinese citizens in Lhasa, thus lessening its depth and meaning, if not negating them, in the eyes of the wider Chinese public audience.[6] What the political and media authorities described as 'smashing, burning, beating, and looting', referring to some violent incidents that had marred the revolt, was dismissed by Shokdung as regrettable but minor compared to five decades of 'smashing, burning, beating, and looting', inflicted by the Chinese state on a large scale upon Tibetans since Tibet's 'liberation'. He also claimed that the revolt was completely unorganised and thus rejected the official version according to which it was carefully planned from outside.

In his book, Shokdung did not only assess the 2008 revolt from a Tibetan point of view, a decentering move that was bold enough: he questioned the ultimate aim of the Chinese government in its handling of minorities. Briefly, he questioned poverty relief in Tibetan regions under the name of development, called the Chinese regime a 'fierce dictatorship', 'autocrats who demand a slave-like allegiance', an 'absolutely merciless régime' and he explicitly talked about 'political repression'. Shokdung also showed little appreciation for the average Chinese citizen: like many other Tibetans, he considers that Chinese people 'prefer to survive like fugitive foxes [and] will find any way they can to carry on living under coercion and suppression', rather than 'die as a defiant tiger' like Tibetans.

The Chinese government and the Chinese man on the street were not the only targets of Shokdung's indictment: he also expressed defiance towards hypocritical Western politicians, showing a lucid analysis of Western opportunistic international interventionism. They would only stand up for a foreign people provided they could gain from it, he wrote, and they could not gain anything from helping Tibet. 'If Tibet turns out to be a treasury of mineral resources below ground and a treasury of medicinal resources on the surface, ... the 990,000-strong righteous and invincible armies of the "yellow haired monkeys" may come, but they would then treat it as an acquired economic asset, just as they have done elsewhere.' His conclusion was thus that Tibetans can only count on themselves and their peaceful struggle to call for a change in the Chinese political system.

The book ended on a chapter called: 'A lesson in the peaceful way to resolve all', opening the debate into political philosophy, in a 'light' and simplified version. In this long chapter, Shokdung introduced the figures of Thoreau and Gandhi and the concepts of non-violence and civil disobedience to Tibetan readers, in simple terms, fulfilling two aims: opening readers to trends of philosophy and world history with which they were totally unfamiliar, and suggesting modes of peaceful action for future movements, because in a rather pessimistic conclusion, Shokdung foresees that, unless the Chinese government takes a more open stance on Tibetan people's claims, more Sino-Tibetan conflicts loom ahead.

It must be underscored here that the book never calls for independence, or separation of Tibet from China. Still, it was later known that Shokdung had been accused of 'instigating to split the motherland,' according to the Tibetan blogger Woeser and her website (inaccessible in China) 'Invisible Tibet.'[7] But Shokdung was released on 14 October 2010, that is, after a six-month detention, and according to Shokdung's lawyer, Li Fanping, he had been 'released on "bail pending trial."'[8] The exile-based group International Campaign for Tibet explained that he was 'allowed to go home under *qubao houshen* (取保候审) terms... *Qubao houshen* literally means to "obtain a guarantor while pending trial" and can be described as non-custodial detention and as a form of probation, since conditions may be imposed on the movements and activities of the suspect, who can subsequently be jailed for violating the conditions.'[9] Indeed, when I met Shokdung the next year, although he had gained back his original position at the publishing house, he had to notify the police in advance of of every move away from Xining. I met him there again in the summer of 2014, busy proofreading a soon-to-be published new Tibetan language novel. His privately-run bookshop, 1+1, had been allowed to reopen. But he still could not leave Xining for more than several days on end without getting phone calls enquiring as to his whereabouts.

Apart from the boldness of its content, its literary style also deserves attention and praise: it flows remarkably well in the Tibetan language, and teems with traditional images, proverbs, and analogies such as 'Mount Meru', 'the nine layers of the earth', 'hungry ghosts', countless cultural references with which Tibetans are familiar. There is no trace of Chinese syntax or political lexicon, which often mars new Tibetan essays and makes them difficult to understand. When neologisms are indeed created for the purpose of this book, such as 'civil disobedience', they are carefully explained and justified, with due respect for the Tibetan language, in the long and well-established tradition of careful translation that Tibetans have emulated since the 8th century when they undertook to translate the wealth of Buddhist literary heritage (mainly from Sanskrit) under imperial patronage.[10] The overall structure of the book is coherent, with clearly delineated headings and sub-headings, in the fashion of traditional Buddhist commentaries.

For all its formal qualities and amazingly brave content, this book may occasionally displease the well-wishing and perhaps naïve Western reader. Shokdung, who is a self-taught political scientist and historian, makes the general and dubious claim that 'the Tibetan psychology is a primitive one, in which many characteristics of pre-civilised peoples can be seen,' and '[Tibetans are] a primitive people still in the clutches of an old-world psychology of demons and spirits'. This ranking of cultures according to their rank of 'civilization' is not accepted in the West anymore, but is still prevalent in China. It is no wonder that Shokdung, having lived in a Chinese environment and read books available in Chinese translation, has to some extent interiorized some features of the dominant gaze. Also, Shokdung does not give up his indictment on Tibetan Buddhism; he claims it does not represent a key contribution of Tibetans to the world, contrary to most people's claims: 'Tibetans have not so far made contributions to world historical progress, political, economic, cultural, or in short, human development'. He still considers strong religiosity, especially Buddhism, as an obstacle to modernity, and not a feature of it. Most Western readers interested in Tibet will disagree of course. Historians might also read with dubiousness the introductory pages, in which Shokdung compares periods of Western intellectual and political history with what was happening in Tibet at that time. In such instances, he falls prey to a fascination that mirrors, in reverse, the idealized perspective that some Westerners entertain towards Tibet.[11] For instance, he writes: '[...] in 1789, when the French made their "Declaration of the Rights of Man", far from knowing about freedom and equality, the Tibetans were ignorant of what the world even was, for that was the year in which Tsenpo Nominhan Jampel Chöki Tendzin Trinlé, who gave them the first rough account of world geography, was born.' This kind of rhetoric does not hold and one could easily imagine a pro-Tibetan essentialist claim to Tibet's superiority by establishing another and reverse dubious parallel between what was happening in the West in 1943–1945 (the Holocaust) and the (relative) peace in Tibet at that time.[12]

But these minor critics should not cast a shadow over the merits of the book. It embodies a turning point in the history of contemporary Tibet an self-assertion and self-narration inside China. Not incidentally, its publication coincided with that of a handful of other equally important books in Tibetan, in Tibet, which all, in their own way, are equally critical of the Chinese 'great narrative' of peaceful liberation, although spanning different literary genres and different times, and which Shokdung incorporates in *Division*. One of them is the 10th Panchen Lama's 'Petition in 70,000 Characters': it was sent by the Tibetan hierarch to Mao Zedong right after the Amdo rebellion and the Great Leap Forward, in 1961. This petition denounced with great courage the folly of Chinese policies at that time. Kept secret for many decades, it was smuggled out of China and translated into English in 1997 and has been available to us since then, but Tibetans had to wait until the late 2000s to read the Tibetan version, which circulated under the counter in Amdo. Shokdung makes frequent references to it, having apparently secured access to it when writing *Division*. Another source Shokdung often quotes is Naktsang Nulo's 'Joys and Sorrows of the Naktsang Boy', a merciless first-hand account of the Tibetan struggle for freedom, its crushing by the all-powerful Chinese People's Liberation Army, and the criminal policies of the Great Leap Forward in Tibetan areas.[13] It was published two years before Shokdung's book and has been banned since then. Jamdo Rinzang's *My Homeland and the Peaceful Liberation* and *Listening to my Homeland* are two illegally-published testimonies (mainly in the form of interviews) of the 1958 Amdo rebellion. They were both rapidly banned and its author was detained and tortured. Another source that Shokdung quotes from is Tsering Dondrup's *The Red Wind Howls* (2009), which is a novel. The use of a fictional source to support historical claims may sound either dubious or unscientific, but Tsering Dondrup's novel was based on archival and first-hand sources. It has been banned since then and the author has been deprived of his position as a researcher at the Henan County archive department (Malho, Qinghai). Shokdung also quotes Theurang, a young intellectual who published a collection of essays, *Written in Blood* and edited a literary journal, *Shardungri*, that also commented upon the 2008 events. Theurang was arrested in April 2010, the same month as Shokdung, and sentenced in June 2011 to a four-year term after he was found guilty of 'inciting activities to split the nation'.

This short but powerful book will open a Western readership to a new phenomenon currently taking place on the Tibetan intellectual scene within China but which, for lack of access to the field and because of the language barrier, has been ignored too long. Tibetans are becoming increasingly articulate and defiant when it comes to expressing their discontent at the Chinese régime, not only as Tibetans but more globally as citizens of a country that has been consistently ignoring their rights for decades, in violation of its own constitution. Along with street protest, it shows that Tibetans within Tibet are developing a 'popular political consciousness and awareness of [their] rights', to quote the present book. These new voices and ideas will be difficult to muffle.

*Professor Françoise Robin teaches Tibetan language and literature at Institut National des Langues et Civilisations Orientales (Inalco, France). Her research focuses on the contents, dynamics and social implications of contemporary Tibetan culture in China, including poetry and fiction, women's writings and the young Tibetan cinema. She has also published translations of proverbs, folktales and contemporary Tibetan literature (*Neige *by Pema Tseden, Paris, 2013), as well as analyses of the current situation in Tibet* (Clichés tibétains, *Le Cavalier Bleu, Paris, 2011).*

TRANSLATOR'S NOTE

ON THE 2008 PROTESTS

Matthew Akester

On the afternoon of 10 March 2008, 49th anniversary of the Lhasa Uprising, hundreds of Drepung monks staged a nationalist protest, marching out of the monastery gate towards the city. They were confronted not far away by a large deployment of security forces blocking their way. They responded by sitting on the ground, creating a standoff, until the police moved to disperse them, arresting dozens.

A few Sera monks staged another protest that day, shouting nationalist slogans outside the Jokhang temple in the heart of the city. They were dragged away, against resistance by the crowd of onlookers, and the following day, hundreds of Sera monks marched toward the city to demand their release. They too were blocked by security forces and dispersed. On 12 March, a similar protest took place at Ganden monastery, further from the city, which was quickly sealed off.

At midday on 14 March, a scuffle between monks from the Ramoché temple and police sparked a major riot. An angry crowd turned on the police in the street outside the temple, who were outnumbered, and soon fled. Rioting quickly spread across the old city. One group of protesters attempting a march from the Jokhang temple down Yutok road to the TAR government compound was blocked by armed police, but security forces were otherwise reportedly absent that afternoon, as rioters attacked government offices and vehicles, and looted Chinese and Hui Muslim-owned shops and businesses. Film footage of rioters destroying property on the streets of Lhasa was swiftly put to use by state media, which claimed that eighteen ethnic Chinese civilians had died in the violence, in a nationwide propaganda offensive invoking racist stereotypes of Tibetans.

By evening, the security forces, Peoples Armed Police and Special Police, moved in. Tibetan witness accounts describe indiscriminate use of force, firing on unarmed protesters and other forms of extreme violence that night, and the following day, when military reinforcements started to arrive from Sichuan. Thousands were detained in house-to-house searches and makeshift detention centres set up around the city, from which reports of torture, denial of medical care and other forms of brutality emerged. These reports have since been substantially confirmed by leaked official video footage and documents, including a police autopsy report.

The Lhasa events were reminiscent of the monk-led nationalist protests that had erupted there in the late 1980s, and returned the Tibet issue to the world stage, but what happened next astonished observers both within the PRC and internationally. Also on 14 March, a monk-led protest march through the monastery town of Labrang, in the north-eastern region of Amdo (some 2000 km from Lhasa), gathered thousands of local people, who converged on the county government buildings, before apparently unprepared security forces dispersed them with tear-gas. A second mass protest the next day was dispersed with the help of armed police reinforcements rushed in from Lanzhou.

Over the following days, dozens of mass protests against Chinese rule flared up in towns and rural areas across eastern Tibet—Machu, Choné, Tewo and Tsoe in Gansu; Rebkong, Chentsa, Mangra, Tsigortang, Chikdril and Pema in Qinghai; Ngaba, Dzorgé, Serta, Sershul, Litang, Kandzé and Tawu in Sichuan, were some of the more frequently cited placenames. Crowds converged on local government offices, calling for the return of the Dalai Lama from exile, and more freedom, if not independence for Tibet, as well as specific demands, such as the release of detained protesters. The five-starred red flag was pulled down and replaced with the snow lion flag, doors and windows broken, walls covered with graffiti, and in a few cases, official property was attacked and burned, as had happened in Lhasa, but the great majority of protests took the form of peaceful marches, sit-ins and candlelight vigils. Numerous sympathy demonstrations were held in schools and colleges, especially by Tibetan student populations in mainland Chinese universities. Altogether, by official count, there were over 150 incidents of protest across the vast area of eastern Tibet in the second half of March.

The state responded to this groundswell of discontent, not unpredictably, with punitive violence. In Ngaba and Kandzé in particular, large demonstrations were fired on by security forces, provoking an intense cycle of further protest and crackdown that would continue for years.

Mass arrests filled detention centres and prisons to well over capacity, reports of horrific brutality were common. Thousands were arrested, many of whom required medical treatment as a result, and hundreds of whom were eventually sentenced, but precise figures remain elusive. Security forces conducted raids on monasteries in affected areas, beating and arresting people and confiscating property with apparent impunity. Police and soldiers deployed in tens of thousands imposed virtual martial law, setting up checkpoints and surveillance posts that made it impossible for people to travel outside their immediate locality, and building military bases next to restive towns, most of which have become permanent fixtures. Monk populations at major centres such as the three great monasteries around Lhasa, and the Ngaba Kirti and Labrang monasteries in Amdo were detained en masse and shipped to detention centres for 're-education', while schools were closed down, and the loyalty of Tibetans in government service tested. One test was sending them out in 're-education teams' charged with drilling the population in official propaganda about the kindness of the Communist Party and the disastrous consequences of rebelling against the Chinese Motherland. This had been common practice in monasteries since the introduction of hardline policies in the 1990s, but had not been extended to society at large since the end of the Maoist era.

The Tibetan plateau was sealed to outsiders, and foreign media in particular, since the outbreak of the protests, and an information blackout imposed. The few details that became known of these events escaped thanks to the wide availability of mobile phones, and the bravery of individuals who used them—despite tight official monitoring of cyberspace—to send out data and images. Some tightly restricted visits were arranged for groups of foreign journalists, but even then, on two famous occasions, monks in Lhasa and Labrang dared to protest on camera, appealing to them not to believe the government's lies. Despite the massive security deployment, the momentum of protest continued until the early summer, and even moved beyond China's borders. The Olympic torch relay held in anticipation of the Summer Games in Beijing was marred by massive public protest in London, Paris, San Francisco and elsewhere, while universities in the USA and other Western countries with overseas Chinese student populations became the scene of acrimonious confrontation between the partisans of both sides.

The background causes of these protests are not hard to identify: Tibetan grievances against the Chinese state are widely and deeply felt. Longstanding political and religious repression had not been ameliorated by the previous decade of rapid state-led urbanisation and economic development. The mining of precious ores and other resource extraction, facilitated by huge investments in transport infrastructure, was ruining local environments without generating local wealth or employment. Improved access to the plateau had also facilitated a state campaign to move pastoralists off the land and into resettlement villages, depriving the majority of a livelihood. The wealth opportunities presented by state spending on urban development were dominated and largely repatriated by mainland contractors and migrant labour, marginalising the rural Tibetan majority. In 2006, Lhasa was connected to the mainland by rail, a triumph of national integration greeted with foreboding by most Tibetans.

The sparks that detonated this sudden explosion of discontent in March 2008, years after visible protest seemed to have vanished from Tibet, are also quite comprehensible in hindsight. The most significant of these, however, was overlooked by international observers and commentators, and even many Tibetans: 2008 was the 50th anniversary of the 1958 Amdo uprising, the bloody suppression of which constitutes the darkest chapter in the history of Tibet's subjugation by Communist China. In the political imaginary of the Exile government and Tibet sympathisers worldwide, the Lhasa uprising of March 1959 is the moment at which China forcibly took control of the country and forced the Dalai Lama to flee. While this is quite correct, the events preceding that moment are not so well known or appreciated. The extension of 'Democratic Reform' (Communist expropriation of 'class enemies' and forced collectivisation) to pastoral areas of eastern Tibet, and the Amdo region in particular, in the spring of 1958, sparked widespread resistance. The PLA responded with a brutal counter-insurgency, military assaults on civilian populations, the destruction of monasteries and communities, and the mass incarceration of survivors, many of whom starved to death in prisons and labour camps. The very words '1958' evoke a sense of collective and still unresolved tragedy for the people of Amdo, which does much to account for the eruption of protest there after half a century of nominal assimilation.

Another spark, one more widely recognised, was Tibetan indignation and despair at the award of the summer Olympic Games to China. The triumphalism of an ascendant China taking its place on the world stage stuck in the throats of the Communist régime's many opponents and victims, none more so than the people of long-occupied and oppressed Tibet. Anecdotal evidence at least points to a collective sense that this was the last chance Tibetans would get to show the world that China still had many wrongs to redress before proving worthy of the kudos of hosting the Olympics—not to mention its universalist and humanitarian values, already much betrayed in the 20th century history of the Games.

There was also the fact that Tibetan figures capable of playing an intermediary role between the people and the state, and articulating popular grievances through authorised channels (what the Communist Party calls 'United Front Work'), had largely been eliminated by the hardline policies of the 1990s. After the defection of the 17th Karmapa (in 2000), and other senior clerics who refused to endorse the Party's candidate for 11th Panchen Lama, soft-power options for reducing tensions in the relationship had dwindled. The cultivation of persuasive spokespersons with local charisma and authority, once considered an essential aspect of 'Nationality Policy', seemed to have succumbed to a more ruthlessly assimilationist agenda.

Against this background, one can understand another of the sparks sometimes supposed to have ignited protest in March 2008: in his annual 10 March address to the Tibetan people that year (banned but nonetheless eagerly spread by word of mouth inside Tibet), the Dalai Lama concluded that his renewed attempts since 2002 to conduct negotiations with the PRC on the status of Tibet had come to nothing. China was not listening, the Dalai Lama said, so he no longer had the confidence to continue to appeal to the Tibetan people for forbearance, with no prospect of hope to offer in return. While not necessarily an incitement to protest, this was nonetheless a bleak message to his people that nothing substantive was being done at the highest levels to address the injustice they suffered.

The outbreak of protest in March 2008, and in particular its wildfire spread across Tibetan areas of Qinghai, Sichuan and Gansu, seems to have come as a rude shock to the PRC authorities. Their immediate response, as already mentioned, was to deploy security forces in large numbers to seal off the plateau and restore order by any means necessary, including disproportionate use of force, mass arrests and tight surveillance of communications. Monasteries, towns and villages where incidents of protest took place were blockaded by armed police and soldiers, who then remained in the area, manning checkpoints along main roads, conducting armed patrols and doing martial arts exercises or target practice to send a message to the inhabitants. This intense security presence has remained in place ever since, at least in the worst affected areas, since the state lacks the confidence or the will to withdraw it.

Then came re-education, not just in the monasteries, but for the population at large. Local governments in all Tibetan areas appear to have been given quotas for conducting re-education in Socialist ideology and law, the evils of the old society and the benefits of Socialism and so-called 'Scientific Development', at township and village level public meetings, and in schools. This often takes the form of screening 'patriotic' films, and making sure that the national flag and portraits of national leaders are prominently displayed in public spaces, institutions and private homes. It also involves classes for ordinary residents held by local neighbourhood committees at which attendance is monitored and points given based on performance. Re-education campaigns frequently require participants to submit written pledges of loyalty to the PRC state and denunciations of the Dalai Lama before completion.

There was also a drive to 'clean up the cultural market' and 'smash rumour-mongering', which means the publication of non-officially sanctioned content, like books, magazines, pop songs and videos that celebrate Tibetan culture and identity without praising the Party and Motherland. This includes not only explicitly political material, such as the present work, but even mildly suspicious songs, poems and images. Dozens of writers, singers and artists have been arrested and sentenced to both administrative detention and long terms of imprisonment since 2008, as have ordinary citizens caught with such material in their possession.

Control of monasteries has always been seen as crucial for 'maintaining stability' in Tibet, and the leading role played by monks and nuns in many of the protests prompted the state to step this up. Management Committees nominally elected by the monastic community were the mechanism used to implement official policy and monitor management of religious institutions since their re-establishment in the 1980s. Now it was decided that these bodies had not been doing their job properly, and should be replaced by directly appointed non-monastic officials. A parallel series of measures emphasising subsidised health care and old age pensions for monks and nuns was announced at the same time, but this too was designed to reward the politically reliable, as part of a campaign to 'select patriotic, law-abiding monks and nuns' and award privileges to 'harmonious and progressive monasteries', meaning those that do not protest.

In the longer term, new Tibet policies introduced in response to 2008 have been concerned with closer control of the grassroots level. The Party seems to have concluded that dissent is endemic in rural areas, and a stronger presence, in terms of administration, surveillance and propaganda, is needed to contain it. In 2011, a three-year campaign of stationing 'work teams' in every village was launched in the TAR, in which cadres from Party and government offices are sent to live and work 'alongside the masses' and, in the words of regional Party secretary Zhang Qingli '...communicate Party policies to them, watch them and thoroughly understand their political thoughts'. Their duties are to 'maintain stability', to strengthen local Party organsations, to educate the population about the 'kindness and warmth' of the Communist Party, and to devise schemes to boost local income. Similar policies have been adopted on a lesser scale in Tibetan areas of other provinces.

Popular protest has of course continued, despite the crackdown: there have been movements to boycott New Year celebrations and spring planting, mass protests against mining, resistance to re-education in monasteries and forced displays of patriotism, and student demonstrations against the downgrading of Tibetan language in education. Some areas like Kandze, Ngaba and Rebkong remain paralysed by tension, and new centres of unrest have emerged in the Nagchu and Chamdo prefectures of TAR. The effect of military repression and intensive surveillance has moreover been to provoke new forms of resistance, such as individual self-immolation protests. The argument made in *The Division of Heaven and Earth* that 2008 marked the emergence of a new determination among ordinary people for popular struggle against 'the dictatorship' has thus been borne out so far. Even the dictators would have to agree, as more than five years later they still describe the 'struggle against the Dalai Clique' (that is, the crushing of Tibetan dissent) as 'complex, acute and protracted.'

Matthew Akester is an independent researcher and translator working in the field of Tibetan history. His published translations include Memories of Life in Lhasa Under Chinese Rule *by Tubten Khétsun, Columbia University Press, 2008.*

PREFACE

I felt three major emotions this year: joy, sorrow and fear. This book will first account for each of these, before going on to explain the ideas of non-violence that they raise. Generally speaking, feelings cannot be communicated literally, for two reasons: first, because there are limits to how we can express them to others; and secondly, there are limits to others' experiences. If the person expressing the feeling is lost for words, or the listener lacks any similar experience, then the feeling cannot be successfully communicated, since feelings cannot be explained in analytical terms. People use whatever names and terms they can find to make their feelings understood, and communicate them through facial expressions, gestures and tones of voice, but literal communication is impossible. From this perspective, the entirety of human knowledge can only ever be expressed through supposedly analytical explanations, or just through simple statements. Accepting that this is the way things are, I will nevertheless try to express my feelings through sheer insistence.

In oral tradition, it is said that long ago in Tibet, moments of joy and sorrow once occurred three times in the same day. It was during the time of the Great 5th Dalai Lama. One day, the bad news came that he had passed away, and the people were struck with sorrow; immediately after this came a report that his reincarnation had been found, at which they were elated; and at the announcement of his enthronement later that day, all were overjoyed. Traditional accounts of Tibetan history are so mixed with fantasies and subjective views that they are hard to believe, but it is recorded that Dési Sanggyé Gyatso kept the death of the Great 5th Dalai Lama secret for more than ten years, due to various external and internal factors;[1] and if we admit that we cannot be sure that such an unusual thing could not have happened at such an unusual time, and adopt the myth for present purposes, I could say that I had experienced three special feelings of joy, sorrow and fear this year, just like the three successive moments of joy and sorrow that once occurred in a single day in Tibetan history.

TERMINOLOGY

'Happiness comes from freedom, and freedom from courage'

Pericles[1]

The peaceful Tibetan revolution of 2008 was named 'the Lhasa 3/14 incident' or 'the Lhasa incident of beating, smashing, looting and burning' by the authorities, whereas Tibetan media and writers called it 'the great peaceful uprising', 'peaceful uprising in the Year of the Earth Rat', 'peaceful rising', 'mass rising' and similar phrasings. I would follow these descriptions, because the names given by the authorities do not reflect the full extent of the events, do not recognise their nature, and are not impartial. Mostly, they are biased rhetorical denunciations, so I reject them.

However, Tibetans have also called this peaceful revolution 'organised and directed', which it was not; 'a protest against the oppressors', when it was more like a full-scale revolt; or 'a common resort to arms against a reactionary régime', when it was actually peaceful: so I will reject these characterisations too.

My preferred wording, since it took place in the Year of the Earth Rat[2] (the 50th anniversary of the 1958 revolt in Amdo); was peaceful in character and revolutionary in nature; and accords with definitions like 'a great transformation of the natural world or society' and 'a replacement of an old social order with a new one, and promotion of social progress', will be to follow Tibetan convention and international usage and call it 'the peaceful revolution in the Year of the Earth Rat'.

BIOGRAPHICAL NOTE

Tra-gya, who uses the pen name Shokdung, is one of Tibet's few secular intellectuals. He is the author of several controversial books and essays on the relation between Tibetan culture and modernity, and until his arrest in 2010 worked as an editor for the Qinghai Nationalities Publishing House in Xining. His pen name, which literally means 'morning conch', might be rendered in English as 'wake-up call'.

BIOGRAPHICAL NOTE

[illegible]

1

JOY

From the vantage point of history, it is truly gratifying to see the Tibetan people, at the start of the twenty-first century, standing up for freedom and equality, rights, democracy and religious freedom on the broadest terms, with sincerity and determination. Whether this peaceful revolution in pursuit of rights is seen overall as a struggle for civil rights, or in narrower terms as a struggle for the sake of one nationality, it is a definite milestone in the history of the Tibetan people. Only servants of the dictatorship would not welcome it; everyone else understands its importance.

In retrospect, it seems that during the past thousand years or so since the demise of the imperial state,[1] Tibetans have devoted all their intelligence and wisdom, their energy and ability to the inner life of the mind, to discovering its nature, and following Dharma and the religious life exclusively. Over that long period, they have surrendered any principles of territoriality and heritage, of domestic governance and bravery from the imperial era, and have dedicated themselves to spiritual perfection on behalf of all sentient beings on the broadest terms, with sincerity and devotion, teaching adherence to the four views of the Four Noble

Truths[2] and the mind training of 'parting from the four attachments', and acting accordingly. For each of the poles of secular culture and religious culture, worldly knowledge and transcendent knowledge, existence and quiescence, the manifest world and the hidden, the former were rejected in favour of the latter, or at least the latter were prioritised and the former relegated. People followed religion, concentrating on the names of the Buddha, Dharma and Sangha, while the secular objectives of freedom, equality, rights and democracy were not pursued. Although the traditional mindset of safeguarding the domestic polity remained from the imperial age, under the system of 'religious and secular authority combined' in which it later ended up, most people did not even know whether secular values like 'freedom', 'equality', 'rights' and 'democracy' were things to be eaten or drunk.

Freedom and equality, rights and democracy and other such principles are fundamentally political concepts, often incomprehensible in a country with little sense of political, territorial or national awareness. The absence of these concepts can be traced by making a chronological comparison with other countries.

In 1215, the English wrote their Magna Carta or Great Freedom Charter, but at the time when those principles were being enshrined, the Tibetans were living in a fragmented polity; with each principality having submitted to Yuan imperial hegemony, they were solely occupied with building new monasteries.[3] Many years later, at the end of the Dark Ages, in the year 1689, when the English again drew up a Bill of Rights, Tibetans were in a state of further fragmentation, arising from disputes between different religious schools. At a time when others, greedy as predators, were waiting to take advantage and engaging both openly and covertly in plots to seize power, the Tibetans were engaged in indecisive conflicts over religious affiliation, as evidenced by Jamyang Shépa Dorjé composing his 'Great treatise on philosophy' at that time.[4]

Then in 1776, less than a hundred years later, the same year that the Americans wrote their Declaration of Independence and announced to the world the rights of man to freedom and equality, Emperor Qianlong invited the famous 6th Panchen Lama Palden Yéshé to Beijing, and without delay (in 1779) he went there to give teachings. The promulgators of the 'Edict of the Year of the Water Ox' (in 1793), restricting the powers of the Tibetan government and affirming the powers of the Ambans,[5] those who turned the order of political affairs on its head, were hailed by the Tibetans as 'supreme', as 'Manjusri in earthly form' to whom they bowed like lost children reunited with their mother. The reason for going may have been to perpetuate the 'priest–patron' relationship, which they claimed was the supreme form of relations between states, but the reality was that the emperors merely handed out seals, titles, ranks and gifts to their subjects. This humble acceptance of invitations, one example of 'priest–patron relations' out of a hundred, clearly signals a relationship of superiority and inferiority rather than one of equality or freedom.[6]

Not many years later, in 1789, when the French wrote their 'Declaration of the Rights of Man', the Tibetans were far from knowing about freedom and equality; they scarcely even knew about the shape of the world. For that was the year when Tsenpo Nominhan Jampel Chöki Tendzin Trinlé was born, the man who gave them the first rough account of world geography. In 1830 he composed his 'Full Description of the World', but this partial account of the geography and populations of some of the world's countries was couched in legend, folklore and fantasy, and sketched from a religious perspective rather than being intelligible in secular terms. So whatever impression it gave Tibetans of what was important and valuable in other countries of the world, its depiction of human freedom and equality in political life cannot have been accurate.[7]

In 1948, after one thousand years of isolation, of dismissing all worldly affairs as mere chaff and prizing religious experiences like gold, Tibet woke up to the United Nations Organisation being established. The Universal Declaration of Human Rights was drafted, according parity of status to all nations and peoples regardless of whether they are powerful or weak, rich or poor, guaranteeing the principles of freedom and equality for all humanity. Finally the Tibetans, who seek spiritual perfection for all living beings, became aware of the rest of the world, and arranged to send a delegation abroad. Like the proverbial patching of a beggar's rags, this amounted merely to organising a 'Trade Representative Mission' with support from the UK and USA, to visit America and some other countries.[8] Thus the land and people of Tibet appeared to stand for nothing and no one in particular, like a fox riding on a tiger's back, at which anyone could aim a kick, and so it has remained until now: a country of nobodies, sitting idle after banging the drum in celebration of their own defeat. (This account of Tibet's history was written with reference to the chronological tables in the 'Great Tibetan–Chinese Dictionary' and 'Dungkar's Encyclopaedia').[9]

From studying this simplified chronology, we might deduce some of the basic features of Tibetan history: a history of repeated capitulation, sectarian conflict, priest–patron alliances and closure to the outside world. Over the period when people in other countries came to recognise the primacy of human nature and to establish the customs and laws of freedom and equality for their own welfare, the Tibetans were stuck in their pursuit of religion, and through seeking protection in the political sphere, failed to secure their own political interests. It seems that Tibet's history can be summarised that simply.

At last, at the start of the twenty-first century, our large-scale peaceful revolution, not just in Lhasa but in all three provinces of Tibet, calls out for freedom and equality, with complete determination and sincerity. It may not appear directed towards individual rights, but it is a sure sign of a new awareness of nationality, culture and territory. This revolution, starting from the 10 March anniversary in Lhasa,[10] was like a stone thrown into a pond, sending ripples out in all directions, provoking demonstrations from monasteries to towns, among men and women, from Tö Ngari in the west to Mé Doekham in the east,[11] from the highland pastures to the valley footpaths, like stars lighting up across the sky or flowers bursting into bloom from the earth.

This new inspiration, like the urge of a wild tiger to take to the forest or a yak to the high mountains, despite knowing the contest to be as unequal as that between an egg and a rock, a sparrow and a hawk, or a goat and a wolf, is like a long-cherished hope falling from the sky like a comet, or a dammed spring finally bursting its banks. Yet that relentless autocracy, which heaps endless cycles of punishment upon us, condemning us to confusion, falsehood and delusion, encircling us with trickery, deceit and lies, prodding us with cruelty, violence and coercion, which starts the day with beating, crushing and suppressing and ends it with undue praise, unjust criticism and accusation, will not hesitate to dismiss us to the hottest or coldest extremes of hell.

But though the truncheon keeps hitting, do not be afraid. White bones may break, but do not flinch. Red blood may be spilled, but do not fight back. The courage to set face and heart against sharp steel, heavy chains and the hail of bullets in defence of the 'sheep's breast' of one's own land, to safeguard the 'golden hammer' of one's own territory, no power can reduce this human courage by the slightest degree.[12] The ferocity of tigers, leopards and bears is driven merely by the need for food, and the fearlessness of a robot is purely mechanical. Although graced by the smiles of the gods and terrorised by demons, this courage of human will comes not from divine blessing or demonic influence, nor can men exchange it at will. It comes from our fathers speaking to us and our mothers comforting us. If Avalokitesvara sees, he can smile down from the peak of Sumeru; and if Amitabha hears, he may laugh from the depths of the ocean.[13] For the poetic image of the 'Snow lion sleeping in the Kailasa mountain of my mind that trembles heaven and earth by shaking his turquoise mane' has now become the 'Skyward-leaping snow lion in the Kailasa mountain of my mind that trembles heaven and earth by shaking his turquoise mane'.[14]

So how does the most awesome of powers make the whole world shudder and yet keep them in their thrall? Some see them as monsters in power, and for these people I see the courage that refuses oppression and seeks to overthrow it as well justified. Some see their oppressors as having greedily stolen what should rightfully be shared, and in their case I see their determination to fight the crooks and bandits who seek to possess every last grain of earth as valid too. Some see their autocratic power as the outcome of the triumph of materialism over idealism, and without getting too mystical, the idea that the power of faith is superior to other kinds of power is also sympathetic. Thus, whether resistance comes from the angle of political coercion and suppression, economic pillage and extortion, or cultural domination, all have contributed to the emergence of this peaceful revolution.

Essentially, from what I have observed so far, I consider the root cause to be the reawakening of a dormant sense of domestic sovereignty resting deep in our psyche since imperial times, as our courage seeking to assert an ethnic and territorial 'self' or identity.[15] I find three main contributing factors: one, that Tibetans even now are not very advanced in political, economic or cultural awareness; two, the majority of the population being committed to religious faith did not actually participate in the revolution; and three, the participants were mainly young people, so one can conclude that, rather than faith, the main factor was the emergence of a fresh courage, produced by the evolution of long-dormant psychological patterns. It appears that most of the brave young people who participated were not the breadwinners of their households, but were those who networked and reacted promptly, who had courage and far-sightedness, commitment to their people and strong loyalty, and once their dormant sense of courage was awakened, the outbreak of such a revolution, the calls for freedom and equality at times and places determined by local circumstance, became inevitable.

Whether history is determined by cause and effect or is naturally fortuitous can be debated endlessly by the world's historians, and I have no particular opinion to express. At first glance, this revolution might look like a sudden incident that came about by chance, but ultimately I prefer to see it as a resurgence of the continuous current of inherited identity and martial bravery from imperial times, in our marrow and in our blood. The idea that this revolution happened simply because of the power of faith seems hard to believe, since not all those with faith participated, so I would rather put it down to the force of courage.

Those taking a world perspective see this peaceful revolution in the Year of the Earth Rat as a continuation of the 'colour' revolutions, and from a global angle this view is fully justified. Since the 'featherdown revolution' or 'velvet revolution' in Czechoslovakia in 1989 peacefully replaced the power of the Communist Party and cooperatives with democracy as gently as down or velvet, a series of 'colour' revolutions took place in east European and central Asian states at the start of the twenty-first century, such as the 'Rose revolution' in Georgia in 2004, which took the rose and the colour pink as its symbol; the 'Orange revolution' in Ukraine in 2004, which took the chestnut flower and colour as its symbol; the 'Tulip revolution' in Kyrgyzstan in 2005, which took the tulip flower and the colour yellow as its symbol; and the 'Saffron revolution' in Burma in 2007, named after the colour of the monks' robes, since opposition to the military government in Burma was led by the monks. These 'colour revolutions' were all aimed at replacing authoritarian or non-democratic régimes, and their participants held flowers to symbolise commitment to freedom and democracy through peaceful means.

If we consider the Tibetan peaceful revolution in the Year of the Earth Rat as part of this global movement for peaceful evolution towards freedom and democracy, the circumstances of it opposing an authoritarian régime by using peaceful methods and seeking freedom and democracy allow us to count it among the 'colour revolutions'; and since the main force opposing the armed forces of the state were monks, and the colour of monks' robes is saffron, it would be appropriate to call it the 'Tibetan saffron revolution'. What I have termed the 'Tibetan saffron revolution', or the peaceful revolution in the Year of the Earth Rat, was one of the main topics of 2008 for the international media, and if it is recorded in world history, even if its objectives have not been immediately met, or victory not immediately assured, then, as they say, 'If it succeeds, that is that, but even if it doesn't, it is still a great thing.' So I judge that the Tibetans made an unprecedented and ineffaceable contribution, in more than mere words or prayers, to the human quest for freedom, equality, rights, democracy and peace.

Tibetans had not staged any major political protest for a long time, and had never had a political uprising, struggle or revolution. To my mind, this is due to three main causes: first, lack of political awareness of their territory and sovereignty; second, lack of concern for anything but religion; and third, geographic dispersal of communities and lack of concentration of population. When people today hear political terms like 'protest', 'uprising', 'struggle' and 'revolution' they tend to recoil in terror, which is the legacy of the Communist revolution, the time when people were branded as 'counter-revolutionaries' and 'bandits' and struggled, were beaten, suppressed, eradicated and branded; the associated sense of terror has still not disappeared. Although that kind of struggle is called a 'struggle' and that kind of revolution is called a 'revolution', violent struggle and violent revolution can in fact triumph through violence, and prevailing through violence is often the natural way. The revolution in the Year of the Earth Rat was a peaceful revolution, peaceful struggle and peaceful protest, a revolution consistent with human values, not a totalitarian revolution, and thus one that people all over the world, in East and West, can approve as great and glorious.

Thus, after careful thought, my reasons for being joyful are four: one, the significance of the revolution; two, the influence of the revolution; three, the objective of the revolution; and four, seeing signs of the truth being ultimately vindicated.

The significance of the revolution

This has five aspects: courage, awareness, revolt, record and message.

1. *Courage*

The revolution signifies the virtues of undiminished courage, the latent bravery of the tiger and leopard-like warriors of imperial times leaping to prominence when conditions demand. Those who joined in the revolution, like avatars of the 61 divisions of braves,[16] the dead, the living and those still in prison, are all war heroes and heroines, and if they embody that ancient bravery, it is because this land is little suited to other ways, being unpacified by a thousand years of the religion of non-self and emptiness, unsubdued by fifty years of political repression and cruel dictatorship. The movement grew from west to east, spreading back from east to west with the awesome power of a mountain shattering into rocks, the chilling splendour of a thousand thunderbolts bursting at once, the roar of a torrential waterfall, a tremor shaking the nine layers of the earth, falling to earth from heaven and leaping to heaven from earth; this vital courage surged forward, flowing with blood, bubbling with purpose in the face of pressure as heavy as Mount Meru,[17] a torment as searing as the hottest hellfire and as bleak as the cravings of hungry ghosts in a reawakening of the fundamental courage of the imperial age.

It was like the upper division of warriors, pitching their tiger tent, like horses killed in battle, faces smeared with blood, resolved not to turn back; or like the middle division of warriors, painting their swords, eating the food offered to the dead, wearing the same sheepskin robe till they die, resolved not to turn back; or like the lower division of warriors, breaking their scabbards, saying last words to their families and giving wives and children to their care, resolved not to turn back, making a pledge with their lives, offering their lives in payment, preparing with solid determination for the road of no return to the goal of freedom and rights, indifferent to joy and sorrow.

The Chinese, meanwhile, are content with merely filling their stomachs; and the 'yellow-haired monkeys'[18] forsake the truth in their quest for selfish gain. But our heroes and heroines of the revolution, whose stories and names will be recorded by historians, have written a new page in Tibet's history; the foundations have been laid for a new pillar inscribing the history of the Tibetans, celebrating the spirit of a people for whom courage is all, individuals animated by courage, with an integrity unbeatable by anyone or anything in this world. How could this picture of supreme warrior courage not inspire joy?

2. *Awareness*

This means appreciating the conduct of domestic affairs and being conscious of their importance. It is the beginning of state, sovereign, political, territorial, national and humane consciousness, and of the awareness of freedom, equality, rights, identity and democracy. For Tibetans, such consciousness and awareness are late in coming, for up to now their consciousness and awareness have been limited to the Buddhas and Bodhisattvas, to all sentient beings, the universal realm, refuge and salutation, the overlord ruler, the works of the divine and demonic, commanding almost their entire attention. The consciousness and awareness of temporal affairs is more universal and all-encompassing, and now the Tibetans are beginning to acquire them.

And now that we are at last developing this consciousness and awareness, the autocrats who demand a slave-like allegiance at all times are realising a new pain and agony, and Western experts who always declared how behind we were in developing national consciousness have had to reconsider. Our 'fellow humans', Westerners who already enjoy freedom and democracy but care little whether others do the same, are put to shame. The Chinese say that under authoritarian rule 'it is better to survive as a fugitive fox than to die as a defiant tiger', so find themselves astounded. Our incarnate Lamas, who have always professed the meaninglessness of cyclic existence, and our scholars, organising state culture departments, have been made redundant. Our officials, the henchmen of dictators and insatiably corrupt, are having a hard time. Our writers, myself included, who pretend to be loyal and sympathetic but are not, have turned as silent as cuckoos in winter. What could inspire joy if not this amazing development of awareness?

3. *Revolt*

This means that this revolution stands for our disapproval of totalitarian rule and our rejection of it. The word 'protest' has much currency in today's written language, but on reflection, it is better to use the word 'revolt' in its older sense here. We revolt against those with concern for their own power and advantage, and no regard for the liberty and rights of the common people, which is characteristic of totalitarianism and absolutism. They operate by deceiving, misleading and confusing the people, and will use force, suppression or intimidation to close off any discontent or challenge to their authority.

It seems to me that there are two ways in which this kind of régime can be put to an end: one is to crush them aggressively with a yet stronger system, as happened with Nazism or Fascism; and the other is to overthrow them peacefully through the united efforts of a population seeking freedom and democracy, like the 'colour revolutions' mentioned earlier. It is hard to see any third way,[19] unless it is the Charter 08 promoted by the Chinese pro-democracy thinker Liu Xiaobo, a 19-point political programme for a democratic, federal China, which managed to get about 10,000 signatures on the internet; but the authorities arrested, detained and called in for questioning those involved, and there is little hope of it being realised.[20] China is said to be in a period of 'peaceful transition' and 'democratisation', and that may be so, but this suggests that until the majority gains political consciousness and awareness of its rights, the appeals of a few intellectuals will not be effective. If the régime does not regard people as human or see life as inviolable, then human rights will not be granted just for the asking, and bringing the totalitarian régime to an end depends on the people developing the determination to do so.

The peaceful revolution in the Year of the Earth Rat can be counted among the second of these two ways and be seen as resulting from the development of a popular political consciousness and awareness of rights; and even if its objectives are not achieved for some time, its significance is palpable. The Tibetan people have not risen in revolt for a long time, and apart from the popular risings at the end of the imperial era,[21] have not staged a political revolt up until now, certainly not in the modern sense of a struggle for freedom, equality, rights and democracy. The year 2008 saw not only a revolt against autocratic rule, but a revolution leading to freedom and democracy, which is highly significant, and what could be more joyful than that?

4. *Record*

This means the significance of registering on the historical record of universal struggles for freedom and democracy. Tibetans have not so far made contributions to world historical progress, political, economic, cultural or, in short, human development. The fact is that they have passed lifetimes and generations profiting only from the achievements of others. If we had to name just one significant contribution, it would be the Buddhist religion, which actually destroyed our imperial dynasty and cut the Mongol empire in half. These days, because Tibetans know something about Buddhist religion, we repeat the feel-good statements that Tibet has 'a brilliant cultural tradition', 'an invaluable religious heritage', 'a great contribution to world peace' and so forth like Mani mantras,[22] and record them on paper like works of art; but in my view, such a conclusion is premature. However, it seems to me that this year's peaceful revolution has added a brilliant and precious new page to the history of humanity's struggle for freedom and democracy. Concerning the fifty years spent by Tibetans disregarding the universal value of freedom, equality, rights, democracy and so on, apart from simply not understanding or becoming aware of their value, it is as Benjamin Constant wrote: 'A people may be overpowered by another, but unless they have seriously erred, they have the possibility to rectify the situation, and when presented with the merest opportunity to succeed, there is no chance that they will waste it.'[23]

When the conditions come good and the time is right, our people have the confidence and determination to give even their own precious lives without regret for the sake of what they want, much as in the past they devoted themselves so much to religion that they neglected the very sovereignty of their country. I may make so bold as to claim that any people or nationality that struggles for freedom and equality, rights and democracy deserves to be counted as a great people or nationality; but if not convinced of this by the arguments of great scholars, who would take my word for it? What I can say is that supposing Tibet were to be destroyed without these aspirations being fulfilled, in the annals of human freedom and democratic struggle it could at least be recorded that at that time, a remote mountain people called the Tibetans underwent hardship, strove with determination and sacrificed their lives for the sake of core human values like freedom and democracy, and thus contributed to the advance of human achievement. I find this worthy and significant, and therefore something to feel happy about.

Another thing to say is that since today the path to freedom and democracy is so broad and even, the options so many and the time so long to make this the most familiar of political systems, if each Tibetan on the progressive path were to chant 'freedom' and 'democracy' along with their Mani mantras, I firmly believe that it would eventually prove effective, even without knowing the exact benefits, just as ordinary people do not know the exact benefits of Mani mantras (but recite them nonetheless in good faith). This is how the Jewish people, after 2,000 years of persecution, beggary, flight, dispersal and loss, in 1948 established themselves in the Middle East and attained the goals of freedom and democracy.

5. *Message*

The peaceful revolution in the Year of the Earth Rat had significant success in sending out a message. For some time after the

10 March anniversary, the world's news broadcasters great and small were full of reports of 'the Tibet situation', 'the 3.14 incident', 'the Dalai' and the progress of the peaceful revolution. Some news channels devoted up to half their output to coverage of the causes of the revolution, its extent, timeline and progress, and at the same time one saw countless discussions, reports, analyses, summaries and images of the revolution reproduced in the media. These were both true and false, straight and twisted, actual and fabricated, but overall at least Tibet received great exposure and informed those who had never seen, heard, known or cared about us, which was a significant plus.

Meanwhile, the official radio and TV broadcasters, newspapers and magazines of the autocracy—the so-called 'collective voice'—reported on how Tibet used to be a hellishly dark slave society and is now a socialist paradise, about the 'crimes' of the Dalai Lama and foreign anti-China forces, the organisation of the exile government and the five NGOs[24] and so on, in documentary style. Chinese, Tibetan and Mongolian scholars, experts, researchers, leaders, Lamas and laypeople were called on to criticise, indict, expose, refute and insult the old 'slave society', and to praise, adore and affirm the present socialist society, to announce that Tibetans were enjoying the most enlightened period in their history, and most of all that the Dalai Lama was 'a beast with a human face', 'a wolf in monk's robes' and other such unprecedentedly overstated and insulting allegations.[25] On the internet one saw moronic Chinese bloggers declare that they had a three-character message for the Dalai Lama: 'He must die', while the political leaders openly took sides, characterising the situation in directly antagonistic terms and resorting to intimidation, declaring that this was a 'struggle over the unity or division of the country', 'a life or death struggle between ourselves and the enemy', and 'Chinese and Tibetans have come to blows before, and everyone knows what the outcome will be (if it happens again).'

Whether in analytical or emotional terms, the coverage of the Tibet situation in both official and unofficial channels within China stopped at nothing, and similarly abroad, with Tibetans in various countries staging peace marches and demonstrations, shouting slogans and presenting petitions, especially during the Olympic torch procession.[26] Tibetans living in free countries used the occasion to publicise the plight of Tibet and its aspirations, and the message spread through agitation across the world to an astonishing degree. In brief, this revolution let the world know that Tibet wants freedom and democracy, and all that was written, photographed, filmed and communicated, true and false, straight and twisted, real and fabricated, served to publicise the situation in Tibet, so that the significance of the peaceful revolution as a propaganda victory is undeniable, and how can that not be pleasing?

The influence of the revolution

This is fourfold: as an example, a warning, a reminder and an encouragement.

1. *Example*

This means providing people living in similar political 'frameworks' or 'households' with a living example of a present-day peaceful revolution, and setting an influential precedent. Tibetans have a saying, 'Better to die defiant as a tiger than to survive as a fugitive fox'; the Chinese have a comparable saying that translates as 'Better to survive as a fugitive fox than to die defiant as a tiger', and these reversed points of view typify Tibetan and Chinese values, and attitudes to life and death, which are in complete opposition. This year's peaceful revolution is a convincing demonstration and practical proof of the Tibetan saying. People living within the same political framework are also under autocratic rule, but those who prefer to survive like foxes will find any way they can to carry on living under coercion and suppression.

According to internal official documents, the number of incidents involving the assertion of rights, including petitions, hearings and even violent confrontations is between 80,000 to 100,000 per year, as can be seen from other sources;[27] but there is less determination for a large-scale revolution in favour of freedom and democracy through protest, demonstrations and uprisings, like this year's events in Tibet. During the 'May 4th movement' of eighty-nine years ago,[28] there were some calls for democracy, but in the many years after that and the passage from one autocracy to another, the issue of ignoring the cost of this form of rule was never resolved, and eventually with the victory of the violent revolution and the cycle of bloodletting, an even more terrifying form of autocratic rule was instituted. With one struggle following another, one crackdown on top of another, in a planned, organised and targeted series of campaigns, people were turned into machines, and tens of millions of innocents sent to their deaths. Not only were there no supporters of freedom and democracy; no one would even mention such things. Far from it, the only sentiment people expressed was 'Long live the autocratic régime!'

That is why a long time passed until 1989, eleven years after 'Reform and Opening Up' (the official phrase coined for the liberalisation of the Maoist order in 1978–9),[29] the time of the 'June 4th incident',[30] in the course of which some freedom and democracy slogans were shouted. But this movement was unhesitatingly crushed by the régime, and therefore aborted, much like this year's peaceful revolution in Tibet. And since then, apart from some pro-freedom Chinese intellectuals, there have scarcely been any protests. By comparison, Tibet's peaceful revolution in the Year of the Earth Rat was large scale, consciously daring, determined and sincere, and thus an example to the 'brothers by the same parents' who prefer to survive like fugitive foxes; since the autocrats will never yield to absolute values like freedom, rights and democracy simply by being asked, struggling to establish them through peaceful revolution is the only way. And this was a living example of peaceful revolution for our times, showing that it is appropriate and necessary to stand up for absolute values. At the same time, it helped to correct the stereotype of Tibetans in official thinking as barbarian, superstitious, wild, uncultured fools; instead we have shown we are a people aware of democracy, rights and freedom, who are not prepared to remain like docile lambs, either dead or alive, under the rule of autocracy. This too makes me glad.

2. *Warning*

This means we are sending a warning to the dictators over their crimes and coercive policies, setting the trend for a thorough change of outlook and behaviour. Since Tibetans came under autocratic rule, their lack of consciousness of sovereignty or awareness of freedom meant that there were no major protests or revolts except the 1959 uprising and the Lhasa riots of 1989, never mind a revolution.[31] Instead they gave the appearance of happily marching to the songs of liberated serfs, following the gradual road to socialism 'like a bird on the wing': however, this peaceful revolution of 2008 is a stern and earnest warning against the crimes and coercive policies of the dictators.

I don't think it's as bad as the dictators treating the Tibetans like animals that they can treat as they please, that cannot snort even if dirt is stuffed in their mouths, cannot scream even if hot embers are poured into their nose-bags, and cannot buck even when fitted with saddles, like carthorses or yaks tamed for riding. Rather it is because Tibetans lack territorial and national consciousness that they were divided and ruled by having their land partitioned between five provinces and autonomous regions.[32]

It is because they lack interest in secular culture and the humanities that all the schools became like monasteries, and all the monasteries get funded to populate themselves with Tulkus.[33] I suppose it is because Tibetans don't care about spoken and written language that we have an education system that will eventually leave us ignorant of our own language, and because we love the philosophy of emptiness and non-self, and love to welcome guests and strangers, that there is a policy of sending large numbers of people to settle in Tibet and 'develop' it. I suppose it is because Tibetans are not interested in rank and office that despite nominal 'autonomy', the senior positions of power are traditionally not conferred on Tibetans, and I suppose that it is because the innermost desires of Tibetans are not to be trusted that access to important positions is closed to them. I suppose it is because Tibetans are content with little, and lazy, that they are given miserly poverty relief grants—meanwhile their resources are being exploited and mined—and I suppose it is because they are naturally wild and barbarian that strict regulation by military threat and intimidation has to be imposed. Such is the onerous rule and coercive policy of the dictators, and ultimately, apart from the greater or lesser degree of force used, the longer or shorter time taken, and the hidden or open manner of conducting them, these principles and policies are in no way unique to Tibet, for everyone knows that it is the eternal aim of excessive power to level the field.

By the same logic with which they control their own people, with no greater ideal than material gain, they have also controlled the Tibetan people up to now; and after fifty years of coercive policies and practices of various kinds fundamentally at odds with the principles of freedom, equality, rights and democracy, the Tibetans staged a revolution with courage and conviction. The outcome is yet unknown, but it has definitely given the dictators something to think about, to understand and get used to, and made inevitable certain changes in their view of, approach to, and policy in Tibet.

In my view, up to now there was no familiarity with or even knowledge of Tibet among the ruling circle; but from now on, if they gain knowledge and familiarity, and discover the magnanimity of political broadmindedness and farsightedness, it could lead on to the democratic path, beneficial to both sides and the universal interest. However, in view of their record, it could well lead to policies and practices more cruel and violent than before, more forceful and vindictive, tight and restrictive, vicious and unrestrained. Either way, this peaceful revolution has sent a sharp warning to the criminal mindset of the dictators, and set a precedent conducive to a change of some kind in all existing views and practices, and this too should be counted among the things that make me happy.

3. *Reminder*

This means impressing on the world that due to the Tibetan people's wishes for freedom and democracy, an incident took place, a serious one at that, and one that must be resolved in some way. In general terms, Tibetans can look to no one other than themselves to resolve troubles or incidents in Tibet. Yet if one thinks in terms of both inner and outer contexts, there is also an undeniable dependence on the outer context, meaning people in the outside world. I usually think of it like this: if two people have a dispute and just quarrel without bringing it to arbitration, there can be no impartial assessment. When they fight and cause injury or bloodshed, then the dispute will go to arbitration, and at that point an arbiter or witness would decide the case, 'without advantaging the thigh or putting out the hip'. With no incident on which to bring a case, how will the Tibetans ever get an arbiter or witness, like those who resolve blood quarrels, as in the saying 'the plaintiffs put their case in the morning but the arbiter decides in the afternoon'. That is why it seems to me that those who say 'The truth of the Tibetan cause will come out in the end', 'Our wishes will soon be fulfilled' and so on are just making prayers to console themselves, because otherwise these are just empty words. This year's peaceful revolution is exactly the kind of incident on the basis of which a case can be brought, and if there is a just mediator in this world, now is the time for them to take such an interest in Tibet and draw up an agenda.

People in foreign countries, however, do not follow the principles of loving kindness and compassion, Bodhicitta, emptiness and non-self, and the exchange of personal happiness for others' suffering, which form the core of Tibetan religion and values. They may have the principles of commiseration with others, caring for their relatives and so on in their own cultures, but this is limited to the idea that 'I will not help others unless there is anything in it for me'; and although they may talk and write about freedom, equality, rights and democracy, it is always prefaced by concern for the 'self'. If there have never been people among them who, like the Tibetans, think of benefitting all beings regardless of their own sovereignty, territory or national identity, there won't be in the future either. If it benefits their 'self', the dictatorships in Iraq and Afghanistan can be overthrown and converted to democracy even if the whole Muslim world explodes with anger; yet if there is no benefit to their 'self', the outside world pays no attention when millions of people are massacred in Rwanda in the cause of ethnic cleansing. When 'self' interest comes first, although help rendered to others in the past may be rendered again in future, this is not the case with Tibet, so unless there is some valuable resource to exploit, such as a large oil reserve, those prepared to help will be few and far between; and although the Tibetan plateau may be considered of strategic importance, in the electronic age oceans and space have overtaken the importance of land mass. If Tibet turns out to be a treasury of minable resources below ground and a treasury of medicinal resources on the surface, as Tibetans like to believe, the 990,000-strong righteous and invincible armies of the 'yellow-haired monkeys' may come, but would then treat us as an acquired economic asset, just as they have done elsewhere.

Whether the truth of Tibet's cause ultimately prevails or not will always depend on the Tibetans themselves, and if Tibetans are to take a firm attitude, things like 'reading the scriptures instead of reciting effective Mantra',[34] saying 'Yes please!' when you mean 'No thanks!', or 'where Jiklo goes, Shiklo follows'[35] are not in tune with reality and not a useful prescription. If Tibetans are to take a resolute attitude, I am sure the rational conclusion is that the time has come for a clear-headed recognition of the forces of evil, and that the day has come to realise how the outside world works.

In any case, this peaceful revolution reminded the rest of the world that the Tibet issue is a serious one, that there is impartial arbitration to be done and resolution to be effected, and this too I find pleasing.

4. *Encouragement*

This means impressing on our own people, in both public and private sectors, and the next generation, an appeal for the importance of the struggle for freedom and democracy. As I have already suggested, the Tibetans abdicated their sense of domestic political responsibility and were silent and closed to the matter for a long period, ignorant of both themselves and others. They have no background of struggling for their own domestic polity, and no history of vigilant defence of the country. In this regard, what they had in their history were just the disputes between religious schools and the vigilant contestation of their monastic estates.

The idea that objectives could not be attained through conflict is related to the spiritual path, and irresolution too is part of the spiritual path. They are born in Tibet out of previous bad Karma, and wander in Samsara because of having exhausted their merit in previous lives. They pray diligently for all sentient beings to have happiness and the causes of happiness, to be free of suffering and its causes, never to lose the state of happiness free from suffering, and to abide in the state of equanimity without bias of hatred or attachment; although all sentient beings have always been in the state of happiness and suffering combined, biased by their attachments and hatreds. Those who dwell on the welfare of all sentient beings are as if endowed with a happiness free of suffering, but those who think of themselves and their people are thereby endowed with suffering. Those who find happiness by cultivating the thought of emptiness and non-self are blissfully at ease, while those with the attachment or aversion to see things as not empty and having self are tense. Conflict is wrong. It is sinful. It is not justified. It is meaningless. Happiness is not being in conflict with anyone or anything.

Thus it is that absence of conflict is best, even conflict for the sake of freedom: the snow lion was eaten away by worms growing inside, until everything it had fell into the hands of others, many tens of thousands of innocents lost their lives, and this is still going on even now. If one is to find what is responsible for the needless death of innocent people, there is nowhere else to look but to the influence of this unacceptance of conflict and struggle. The cultural idolisation of impartial equanimity must, I think, take responsibility for the historical fate of the Tibetan people.

However, by stiffening their courage, broadening their awareness and starting on the road to freedom, the poor Tibetan people need no longer have regard for such ideas. With religion and culture as their background, but freedom and democracy as their goal, the cause they carry forward is their own, and they do it with dignity, putting themselves in the line of fire, putting everything at stake, paying with their lives. This courageous, determined and irreversible revolution has shown Tibetans, whether here or in exile, whether public servants or private citizens, and above all the next generation, the aim and direction of our future struggle, and has created a powerful impact, encouraging them to take the road to democracy and freedom, which fills me with happiness and joy.

The objective of the revolution

This should be the universal human values of freedom and equality, rights and democracy. This is the primary objective, and must also be the secondary and tertiary, and indeed the final objective. It was for this final objective that, over many centuries, peoples riding the battle horse of bravery, nationalities joining with committed comrades and intelligent individuals put their lives on the line, shed sweat and blood and risked their own welfare, with a hundred efforts, a thousand labours and a hundred thousand hardships; and from this year, we too have started on the way to this final objective.

Regardless of place, time or situation, the words freedom and equality, rights and democracy will gladden the heart, will never age or rot, get defiled or exhausted, decline or wither, break, fall or disappear. They are by nature without beginning or end, completion or depletion, increase or decrease, creation or destruction, being or non-being. Regardless of place, time or situation, the qualities of freedom and equality, rights and democracy are justified and guaranteed, sacrosanct values of universal application, and if we speak of truths and standards, there can be none other than these. This ultimate 'green pasture', contravening and violating nothing in the ways of the world, the aspirations of humanity or the fate of individuals, must be the singular objective of this peaceful revolution.

Otherwise, if it is about religion, culture, faith and good intention, this could demean the dignity, value and significance of the revolution, and curtail its trajectory, duration and continuity. Because religion and culture are naturally mutable, as are faith and good intention, and mutable things have no fixed course or conclusion, they cannot be relied upon either. So if the revolution is undertaken for the sake of such things, its continuity, duration and parameters are hard to configure, and the dimensions of its dignity, value and significance also become hard to define.

Therefore it is fitting to declare that the revolution in the Year of the Earth Rat, uniting all Tibetans, monks and laity, young, adult and old, aims to realise universal human values, for this is something easily understood by those on the outside, and requires no further explanation. To say this is to visualise a future, so that one day such a glorious epoch may come to be, and this too gives rise to feelings of happiness in me.

Signs of the revolution's ultimate vindication

This means that in the revolution of the Year of the Earth Rat we can see signs of the truth of the Tibetans' cause being vindicated and of their wishes being fulfilled. In the process, I have also seen signs that my own wishes might be fulfilled. The signs are that 2008 was a major turning point in Tibetan history, one with more positive significance than others and with the characteristics of a rise in fortune. For a thousand years, everything in Tibetan history, whether good or bad, came from religion and religious orders, Lamas and Tulkus, so that the loss of countless lives and having to undergo endless hardship and losing our freedom must also be the result of those people and their way of thinking. Since the Tibetan people have to experience the outcomes determined by the course of their history, they too should have responsibility for forging it. So even if I stir them, shake them up, raise doubts, argue with them or refute them, that is the fact I come up against, and seeing the result, I went after the cause.

Whether or not this is a turning point or a change of direction in Tibetan history depends upon that idea and the people upholding it, for no one else has that capacity. As a writer, I know that writing is of no use whatsoever to the Tibetan peoples' history, and is utterly incapable of providing them with material sustenance. I know that apart from a very few works, like *Common Sense* by the English writer Thomas Paine, literature does not contribute much to the progress of human history.

Nevertheless, the question of who it is that makes human history is a matter of debate. Is it famous people and clever individuals, or is it the mass of the people? To say that history is made by ideas is difficult to prove. But I am an exponent of ideas, and although it may be bias and partiality on my part, or heresy and hallucination, I want to argue that ideas do indeed make human history. Because while freedom and democracy have been explained here as universal human values, once an individual or a people is convinced by the idea of freedom or democracy, they are sure to make their history progress towards freedom and democracy. Seeing things from the perspective of ideas, I see this turning point in the history of the Tibetan people as related to ideas, for when any powerful individual comes to understand universal values like freedom and democracy, the common people also gain in courage and awareness, and their progress on the path to freedom and democracy is begun. But if this does not happen, then such a history will obviously not come about. This applies throughout human history. Without the circulation of ideas from powerful or eminent levels of society, there can be no engagement with specific situations or events in the making of human history. I propose then, overall, that ideas are fundamental to the making of human history.

With regard to the Tibetans in particular, freedom should be divided into the outer aspect of rights and the inner aspect of ideas, and equality and so forth should be similarly divided. I am someone who is lacking in courage and bravery, who blows bubbles of talk, not one who mines the seam of practical action; I annoy people by preaching the inner freedom of thinking and ideas, while casually neglecting the hard graft for political and popular freedom, like the 'dim-wit who is the first to gossip and the old bird that is the first to crow'. But even now, I don't find it wrong or mistaken or deluded to make people upset, angry and impatient by stirring, agitating and revolutionising from the heights of the intellectual, the depths of the conceptual. As a starting point, the growth of awareness of freedom, equality and rights in the inner dimension of ideas must precede all other actions, in time and in all other respects, because ideas are the foundation of all freedom, equality and rights, and thus of greatest importance.

Compared with the outer struggle for rights in this year's peaceful revolution, the inner struggle for rights may lack glitter and brightness, colour and brilliance, core or substance, but in the long run it has to be talked about. For if the goal of the outer struggle is won but the inner goal is not, there will be no difference from the previous autocracy; so talking about these ideas is essential, certainly for Tibetan society and psychology. For anyone with a long-term perspective, there is no contradiction between the outer and inner revolutions: they complement each other, and one might say that flying with this pair of wings is the way to get one to the distant paradise of freedom. By uniting the outer and inner aspects of freedom, we will see the emergence of a fully rounded humanity, a humanity with backbone, with developed potential, and that is basically what I hope for.

I see the signs not just of a glimmer of new dawn in Tibet, but of a new day long and full, in which the Tibetans are like a people 'of fortunate destiny in the midst of evil destiny', beginning a struggle for freedom and rights, joining outer action and inner thinking, with unshakable resolve. And considering history overall, this redoubling of our energies as a new day dawns on the mountain peaks, this again gives me cause for joy.

My writings are not like the religious histories, biographies and autobiographies laced with deceit, falsehood and delusion with which Tibetans mislead their fellow Tibetans these days; nor are they like the writings produced by 'research projects' examining material advantage, reputation, comfort and approval with which Tibetans torment their fellow Tibetans these days; nor are they like the fictional compositions fluffed up with empty falsehoods with which Tibetans numb their fellow Tibetans these days; and this gives me particular satisfaction.

2

SORROW

SHACKLED BY THE MANIFOLD CHAINS OF REPRESSION

The universal values such as freedom and equality, rights and democracy have come to form the basic ideal and objective of all nations, regions and peoples in today's world. This ideal is seen as an optimum standard applicable to all humanity, and hence called universal. In pursuit of this apex of the human world, this Nirvana-like goal, people with concern for governance and strong insight into the human condition have struggled, striven and even fought life and death battles, whether individually, collectively, as parties or public bodies, from generation to generation.

A system taking those universal values as supreme is called 'democratic', and a government that protects those values is called a democratic government. They are bound by the democratic principles that all are equal before the law, that power is held by the people, that elections are equal and impartial, that legislative and executive branches of government are separate, that minorities respect the sentiments of the majority and the majority safeguards the sentiments of minorities, that a people decides its own affairs and so forth, and that freedoms including the freedom of the body, freedom of speech, freedom of belief, freedom of assembly, freedom of association, freedom from absolute poverty and freedom from fear, and equal rights including the right to life, right to equal treatment, equality with regard to social origin and equal property rights be respected in practice as well as in word and on paper. 'Democracy' means nothing other than a system of this kind that protects and guarantees these rights of the individual. In countries with democratic systems, these universal rights are protected as carefully as a person protects his eyes, so that they apply to all equally and are not compromised or exchanged, and peace and mutual coexistence are enjoyed there.

Put another way, when a traditional hierarchical oligarchy becomes aware of universal values and struggles and strives to achieve them, their reward is 'the worst form of government except for all the others that have been tried' (as Winston Churchill described it), a democratic system that takes responsibility for all the rights of its citizens. The origin of such systems goes back to the Greece of the pre-Christian era, but this was just a seed which did not at first spread to humanity as a whole. It was another 2,000 years before it took root with the drafting of the Bill of Rights (England, 1689), the Declaration of Independence (America, 1776) and the Declaration of the Rights of Man (France, 1789), and then it grew. The twentieth century saw the introduction of the United Nations' Universal Declaration of Human Rights (on 10 December 1948):

> a common standard of achievement for all peoples and all nations, to the end that every individual and every organ of society, keeping this Declaration constantly in mind, shall strive by teaching and education to promote respect for these rights and freedoms and by progressive measures, national and international, to secure their universal and effective recognition and observance, both among the peoples of Member states themselves and among the peoples of territories under their jurisdiction.

This carefully worded proclamation to all nations expressed many universal principles, uniting the temporal aspirations of humanity. The boundless promise of the Universal Declaration can be seen as humanity's universal recognition of absolute values. All who live in this world are thereby afforded protection from the misery of absolute poverty, mortal fear and unnatural death. At the present time there are said to be 119 governments in this world that honour these values and put them into practice: the US foreign policy expert Michael Mandelbaum has noted that in 1900 no more than ten nations in the world could be considered democratic; that number had risen to thirty by the middle of the century, and did not change over the next twenty-five years; but by 2005, of the 190 nations in the world, 119 could be counted as democratic. This number does not include Montenegro, which became, by democratic means, a free and democratic state in 2006; and this year, in 2008, Kosovo became an independent democratic state; also Bhutan, a neighbouring country that shares our cultural traditions, was guided towards democracy by its hereditary monarch. If they are counted, it brings the number of democratic countries in the world to over 62 per cent of the total. So the democratic order enshrining universal values is steadily growing, and the success of this democratic political order based on universal values is as clear as the dawn for all to see.

Now the UN Declaration and others like it do not have the force of law in any country, yet as these rights have come to be understood as universally applicable and a fundamental given, the principle that 'Human rights supersede the sovereignty of nations' (Vaclav Havel) has become established; aware individuals and governments with respect for truth and ethics everywhere guard these universal values, along with their lives, as carefully as their eyes, and urge their adoption in other countries. What this tells us is that these universal values have become basic, core values in human societies in today's world.

However, even in today's world there are governments and political parties that disregard universal human values and trample on them, peoples who invade other peoples' territory and deliberately subject them to abuse. There are quite a few governments and political parties that use the name of democracy ('Peoples' democratic dictatorship' etc.) but are actually totalitarian régimes that exterminate, manipulate and control peoples other than their own. In particular, we commonly see and hear about governments and parties that take great pride in putting national sovereignty above human rights, disregard universal human values in favour of national interests, and systematically murder and eliminate those who fight for and support those values. The Tibetans are in just such a position, having long ago lost their sense of domestic sovereignty, lacking territorial, national or sovereign consciousness, and never having had a worldview based on universal values like freedom and equality; they have spent half a century under the control of an autocratic political system of that kind.

Generally speaking, in this world, tens of thousands of lives have been lost in the struggles of peoples for their territory and interests, and there have been life and death struggles too in the cause of universal values. In striving for their rights and for the recognition of certain values, many peoples have in the past fought long battles, and eventually succeeded in winning freedom, and there are many who continue to wage such struggles too. In the historical line of peoples gaining political awareness of the quest for freedom, the Tibetans are latecomers, very slow to awake, very late in reaching conviction and very lethargic. By comparison with peoples that gained political awareness early on, the Tibetans are like retarded fools.

Nevertheless, by the start of the twenty-first century, this people as if ripe on the outside but unripe on the inside, or as if undeveloped from a natural personality to a collective personality, finally gained conviction for freedom and equality, and awareness of the struggle for rights and power, which is a cause of some delight, as already stated in Chapter One. What is so sad is that they did not awake from their dreamlike entrapment in the delusory world of religion and religiosity until now, and having done so only at this late hour find themselves in the grip of an absolutely merciless regime; and in the struggle for rights and power against such an adversary it is terribly, overwhelmingly sad that they will be forced to pay with tens or hundreds of thousands more lives.

The time has now come for us to learn all the things our predecessors did not want to know about, for it is vital that we think through and gain a sense of historical retrospect, a critical perspective on culture, a clarity in political understanding, a sophistication in matters of livelihood. One particularly timely aspect of political understanding is to understand the nature of totalitarianism. What earlier generations called the 'Gongma' as in 'emperor', known to ordinary folk as 'Gongma-tsang' [in Amdo dialect], actually means 'dictator' or 'absolute ruler'. This needs a little explanation.

The nature of totalitarianism

'Totalitarianism' (*wangta gérchö ringluk*) is translated from the Chinese (极权专制主义, Ji Quan Zhuan Zhi Zhu Yi) and is a combination of the terms 'absolutism' and 'authoritarianism'. The former term refers to a modern political system in which power is concentrated in the hands of an individual or group with an ideology or practice of autocratic rule. It is a system that uses the monopoly on power to control all the physical, verbal and mental capacities of citizens and to dominate all aspects of society without exception. An absolutist government keeps an autocratic hold on all political, economic and cultural activity, as well as on the intellectual and spiritual lives of individuals, and goes to the extreme of using violence to enforce this control. The latter term means a system in which the power holders exercise exclusive decision-making power on the basis of force.

The Chinese scholar Hu Xi[1] enumerated the characteristics of totalitarianism in 20 points:

1. Pursuing an exclusive nationalism with the intensity of religious faith
2. Holding state power through a political party run with quasi-military discipline
3. Suppressing with force all publicly expressed opinions contrary to the government
4. Subordinating religious faith to the official ideology of nationalism
5. Venerating the president or supreme leader as divine, and making him the supreme object of faith
6. Promoting the denigration of analysis and information, pandering to and manipulating the uneducated public, and harshly punishing the expression of genuine and honest views
7. Banning or destroying books and misrepresenting the facts of history and science
8. Denigrating scientific and other intellectual enquiry devoted to objective truth alone
9. Replacing argument and debate with the forceful imposition of one-sided views, and party control of news broadcasting
10. Isolating the public from exposure to ideas and communication, and screening the inflow of current information from outside
11. Control of all forms of art and culture by the party
12. Destroying political aspiration and misleading the public with deceit and hypocrisy
13. Active and systematic engagement of the Party in crime

14. False accusation and abuse of those branded 'enemies of the people' by public meetings
15. Reinstatement of primitive forms of justice, and prejudice against those branded 'enemies of the people' and those close to them
16. Constant war preparedness and militarisation of the public
17. Enlargement of the population through a variety of devious methods
18. Indiscriminate indulgence in 'proletarian revolution against capitalism' in all circumstances
19. Suppression of all industrial strikes and protests, and eradication of all workers' movements
20. Control of all professions, industry and commerce by heads of powerful associations

Hu Xi's list of 20 characteristics, elicited for a study by an American political scientist, was given in a speech delivered at a US university in 1941, and reflects the characteristics of the totalitarian régimes in the world at that time, although some of these changed according to circumstances. For instance, 'Enlargement of the population through a variety of devious methods' later became 'Control of the population through a variety of devious methods', as in China's family planning laws. Still, this is a more or less thorough list.

There is another list in six points:

1. Requiring of each individual an attitude of absolute respect for authority
2. No more than one mass political party
3. Rule of intimidation by the party or secret police
4. State monopoly of mass media
5. Use of modern technologies for the control of bodies and minds
6. State control of the economy

These characteristics are so familiar to us from experience that they require no further explanation. Not that they are the only ones, for each observer and analyst may have their own way of categorising and summarising. Such régimes are said, for instance, basically to 'pay no attention to long-term goals but are interested only in short-term fixes, treat the symptoms but not the cause, broadcast good news but not bad news, and ultimately put about distortions and lies, serving their own interests in the name of serving the public interest' (from Bapa Puntsok Wanggyé's *A Tibetan Revolutionary*).[2] And again, 'they love discord, they love to do things slapdash, they love praise, they love to find fault in others, they love to stir up trouble, and whatever happens, they love to beat people up' (from the 10th Panchen Lama's 70,000 Character Petition).[3] It would be hard to summarise all the enumerations of characteristics, but I would like to add two more, based on our own experience: one being the suppression of individuals, and the other the elimination of peoples other than their own.

On the basis of his experience, this writer proposes a fivefold characterisation of totalitarianism, one which is easy to remember: one is having the principle of one party and one system, two is the suppression of individuals as a matter of course, three is the policy of controlling expression and keeping the public in the dark, four is holding power by military force, and five is wiping out peoples other than themselves.

The first point means one party ruling autocratically, not giving any other party or group the chance to hold power, which individual citizens are obliged to revere and obey, the glorification of a singular political model and the banning of alternative groups and beliefs, or the principle of one party and ideology holding absolute power. For instance, under the rule of the Nazi, Fascist or Communist parties, their ideologies were held to be fundamental, and libertarianism and individualism suppressed.

The second point refers to disregarding and trampling underfoot the rights of the individual, and treating individuals as slaves or machines subordinate to larger identities such as state, nation or class. The reason for doing so is to prevent any threat to their hold on power. For instance, the unjustified insistence that individuals throw away even their lives for the sake of 'the Chinese people', or 'the proletariat', or 'the people', 'the common interest' etc. with complete disregard for their rights and in negation of freedom.

The third is removing the freedom of expression, restricting speech and controlling news, communication and the written word so that apart from hearing about the greatness of the ruling party and its achievements, the public are not exposed to real news, and broadcast media including radio, TV and newspapers present a continuous, orchestrated procession of distortions and lies, leaving people confused and in darkness as a matter of deliberate policy. For instance, the load of highly misleading, vacuous talk and ideas about 'socialism', 'communism', 'dictatorship of the proletariat', 'liberating humanity from its chains' and so forth.

Fourth, 'rule' or 'rulership' is a term that means, for them, the exclusive preserve of dictators or an autocratic government, not something open to democratic principles. Possessed by the philosophy of armed confrontation, with blind faith in the power of violence, they rule by force and persecution, and the public are made to live in terror and awe of anything 'political', scared witless by violence, what might be termed 'terrorism by paralysis' or state terrorism, and what they call 'slaughtering a goat to scare the sheep'. For instance, the murder and driving to death or suicide of tens of millions during the whole succession of campaigns like the Land Reform campaign, the Trade and Industry Reform campaign, the Religious Reform campaign, the Anti-Rightist campaign, the Great Leap Forward, the Great Cultural Revolution and so forth.

Fifth, out of racial supremacism and superiority, the autocrats deploy troops, spies and armed police to exterminate other races using violence, as well as peaceful methods involving culture, education, birth control, poverty aid, divide and rule and so forth, to achieve the same end. Since their abuse of power knows no limit, they use methods both peaceful and violent, long-term and short-term, open and hidden, to scatter, destroy and eradicate other peoples. For instance, the murder of millions of Jews by the German Nazis, the massacre of tens of thousands of Chinese by the Japanese Fascists, the extermination of tens or hundreds of thousands of non-Russians by the Soviet Communist Party, and the killing of countless people of other nationalities, including the Tibetans (the number of Tibetans killed is said to have exceeded one million) by the Chinese Communist Party, as well as the assimilation of countless others through all kinds of nefarious methods.

Of course, the defining characteristics of totalitarianism cannot be summarised in just five points, but here I have selected the most relevant points from the classifications of the political scientists mentioned earlier, keeping three of them (points one, three and four) and adding two (points two and five) from experiences that fit with the general character of totalitarian régimes, to come up with these five, just as something easy to remember. So these points about the willingness to take life and shed blood, characteristic of the minions of the lord of the death despatched on earth, are characteristic of totalitarianism, and in the final analysis, the failure to refrain from such chilling savagery, being oblivious to universal human values, even in this day and age, typifies those who serve the interests of a ruling clique and its hold on power.

Thus, two centuries have passed since humanity started out on the road towards meaningful democracy and freedom, sixty years since the defeat of Nazism and Fascism, and sixty years since the

Universal Declaration of Human Rights, yet Communist autocrats can still sign up to international agreements like the International Covenant on Economic, Social and Cultural Rights, the International Covenant on Civil and Political Rights,[4] the International Agreement on Eliminating all Forms of Racial Discrimination and so on, breaking their word and violating their commitments, deceiving and misleading the international community again and again, year by year, beyond all belief. And likewise, at the start of this twenty-first century, when the meek Tibetans staged a peaceful protest calling for universal values like freedom and equality to be respected, those inured to rule by violence responded with troops and armed police and automated weapons, heedlessly and with unlimited force, killing and beating, confining and imprisoning, in a manner unbearable to contemplate let alone physically endure, their crime so grave that even the sky cannot encompass it.

According to the initial Tibetan estimates I have seen, over 120 Tibetans were killed by the dictatorship in the course of the peaceful revolution, over 1,000 disappeared, over 190 were falsely indicted by the courts, and over 6,500 detained. Later, I saw higher estimates of 219 dead, 1,294 seriously injured, 6,705 detained, and 286 prosecuted, but I suppose these are just rough estimates, and it is hard to say whether they are accurate. There is a major discrepancy between these and the initial estimates given by the dictatorship of 953 detained and 76 prosecuted, but this is not the first such discrepancy. Tibetans claim that over 1.2 million Tibetans were killed, imprisoned, sentenced or disappeared by the régime,[5] whereas I have seen some Chinese scholars writing that the number of Tibetan dead was less than 100,000 according to the leadership's internal documents. It is hard for someone like myself to say which side is telling the truth or not, but here are some of the accounts: 'Many hundreds of thousands went to their deaths, and the corpses of prisoners were too many to be buried' (70,000 Character Petition);[6] and 'It was evident from households in the more seriously affected regions that only women, the elderly and young children were left' (70,000 Character Petition); and 'It seems that roughly 20,000 Tibetans, monks and laity, were killed at that time. Those from Kyépur who threw themselves into the Machu river [Chinese: Huang He, Yellow River] were uncounted, but at any rate it is certain that tens of thousands died' (from Jamdo Rinsang's *My Homeland and the Peaceful Liberation*).[7] These indicate that the Tibetan estimate certainly seems warranted, if not actually conservative.[8] Anyway, the turning of the wheel of killing and bloodshed that made Tibet like the lord of death's slaughterhouse, like a hellish prison, like a punishment ground in hell, like a terrifying battlefield is something that 'the sky cannot conceal, even though the earth does', so let us consider each of them in turn.

The lord of death's slaughterhouse

This time too, just as in the past, they branded this peaceful revolution from the very outset as 'beating, smashing, looting and burning', using deception to keep the uninformed public in the dark, and clouding the perceptions of the rest of the world by barring foreign reporters. They turned white into black, and made the alleged violence of protesters the focus of blame and the excuse for their violent repression, opening the way for the three crimes of killing, chopping and quashing; and the other three crimes of beating, crushing and suppressing. Starting with the 10 March anniversary,[9] as this peaceful revolution spread across Tibet like flowers blossoming one after the other, those who shouted slogans, flew flags and joined demonstrations for the sake of their own freedom and beliefs were rather warrior heroes and heroines, with the strength of tigers: visibly so, to see their courage, and tangibly so, to experience it. Innocent wild deer massacred by the guns great and small of the enemy horde, swirling thick as dust, yak, sheep, goats and pigs to the slaughter, or a pile of beans all scattered, this is how citizens, armed with not so much as a needle, were smeared with crimson blood. Old monks called to each other, but no answer; a young boy called to his parents, but no response; parents called to their children, but no reply. Those left behind were numb with shock, even though their chests were split in two. In the oblivious calm that follows the instant destruction of the world, the painless haze that follows the heart being torn out, they disposed of the corpses as if they were dead dogs, dragged them away like sheep carcasses, discarded them like dead insects, making a mockery of the Buddhist belief in the 'precious human body'.

As this hidden realm of the human world, embodiment of ten million wonders, this Tibet, known as the last pristine land on earth, became a twenty-first-century slaughterhouse, none of the peoples of the world came to our aid; even the Dharmapalas and protectors, the territorial spirits and local deities on whom the Tibetan people rely, the Dakas and Dakinis, none intervened to avert disaster and terror.[10] Did humans like myself raise doubts or objections? What I have descriptively called the lord of death's slaughterhouse, has there ever been such a massacre, covering the entire Tibetan plateau? Not to die but to have to keep living through the direct experience of this slaughterhouse, how to survive this other than with the fatalistic expression used by Tibetans, 'Karmic destiny'. 'By light of day there is no outlet for grief, nor for cries of woe in the dark of night, the helpless bereaved seeking solace is all there is.'

How about the cycle of slaughter unleashed in Tibet fifty years ago? From even a glance at the following accounts, we can see how Tibet was turned into the lord of death's slaughterhouse in the past. In his autobiography of *A Tibetan Revolutionary*, Bapa Puntsok Wanggyé wrote:

> Not only was I imprisoned, but those involved in my case, including my younger brother Tubten Wangchuk, who spent 14 years in prison, my wife Dzélek-la who died as a result of mistreatment, and our children were also imprisoned and forced to do Reform through Labour for many years (the eldest son Punkham was imprisoned for six years). Due to this, my kind father Goranangpa Yeshé eventually died tragically of grief and bitterness, and dozens of our relatives were also imprisoned in connection with my case. My fellow fighter comrade Topden and others also died from abuse, and comrade Ngawang Kelsang was imprisoned and forced to do Reform through Labour for 16 years.[11]

In Jamdo Rinsang's *Listening to my Homeland*, Aku Yampel recounts:

> When I got out of prison, I found that my eldest brother Lumbum Chuk, the next brother Taklha, the next one Sanggyé Kyab, and sisters Druk Kyi and Gyamo Kyi had all died in the Laogai (Reform through Labour prison) in Guinan Xian (county). Another brother, Gebha, was killed during the massacre of the Bonkor nomads and others in Kyépur. Only our mother and sister Lhamo Tar were left.

Looking at these accounts, there is not much more to say. From one particular instance, we can get the general picture, we can see that tens of thousands of households must have gone through the sufferings of the lord of death's slaughterhouse.

The hellish prison

Thousands and thousands of people were driven into prisons like sheep, innocent people mown down like hay, rolled like paper, kneaded like hide, crammed into the dark recesses of dungeons; bound with steel wire when there were no handcuffs and leg irons left; their socks and belts confiscated; made to wear black hoods; subjected to wooden and iron clubs and mechanical and electrical punishment devices, a degree of torment possible only in the worst of hells. It was not a matter of just getting knocked about; with deliberate malice, they went for the genitals of those who father the next generation, the laymen, and for the vital organs of those who do not, the monks. The henchmen of the lord of death made threats like spitting bile: 'These guns of ours are made to kill you Tibetans. If you take a single step I will shoot you dead, and your corpse will be thrown on the rubbish heap' (the words of the Labrang monk Jigmé, as reported on the website of the Voice of America's Tibetan language service).[12] Destroying people's dignity by hanging them upside down from the ceiling and stamping on their foreheads is something one might expect to see only in a film about Fascist or Nazi atrocities. Never mind that 'Chinese prisoners are allowed to learn literacy, but Tibetans are not ... Tibetan prisoners are only allowed to speak to each other in Chinese, not in Tibetan ... not allowed to speak their own language or to express their own identity' (from Jamyang Kyi's *A Sequence of Tortures*),[13] even to describe being deprived of sleep during days and nights on end of interrogation to break the will, and the physical beating, hitting and lashing, these three, could barely match even a small fraction of the torment.[14]

As we read in Te'urang's *Written in Blood*,[15] 'The hardest thing to endure is not the physical torture but the invasion of one's thoughts'; and in Jamyang Kyi's *A Sequence of Tortures*, 'One day during interrogation, the thought suddenly came to me that, rather than go through this, I would prefer to be shot dead with a single bullet. My family and relatives might be upset, but for me at least it would be over and done with', this is the kind of torment one would rather die than endure, and under this constant, unthinkable torture, many brave Tibetan souls with the limitless courage of the imperial spirit were broken and maimed, and came to the end of their lives. The torture of deprivation of food and water, designed to turn them all into hungry ghosts, drove people to the edge of life and death, and for those not finished by hunger, the torment of thirst led 'more than 60 among us to drink their own urine' (from Gartsé Jigmé's *The Courage of the Emperors*, vol. 1).[16]

This inhumane brutality of torturing people through hunger and thirst is no different from the past. Not only did innumerable people die of hunger, for the living too:

> with the flames of the suffering of hunger blazing bright, even things like Bacha [the cake residue of pressed oil seeds] and Pukmá [the chaff of harvested grain] which used to be given to horses, donkeys and cattle became like nutritious food and hard to obtain. To maximise the amount of food and relieve hunger, those running communal kitchens used to quite openly pick not just edible grasses but inedible tree bark and leaves, grass roots and grains, and after processing them, mix them with a little food grain and make a kind of slop like pigswill, which they fed to people. Eventually, when even this became limited, there was not enough of it for people to eat to satisfaction. (70,000 Character Petition)

Thus when the torments of hunger passed beyond all limits, those in prison were said to have 'grown a tail' (i.e. become like herbivorous cattle, a term taken from Tsering Dondrup's *Raging Red Wind*).[17] Even worse things happened, for example:

> During the 1958 famine, since he was a 'hatted'[18] reactionary, he was given the job of carrying out corpses. One day, one of his friends who was about to die of starvation asked him to bring back some human flesh when he went to dispose of the corpses. He tried once or twice, but could not find any flesh to bring back, because the dead were people who had also died of starvation, and their bodies were just skin and bone, with no flesh at all. One day, he found a body with a little flesh on it and brought some back. Next day, that person told him 'That meat you brought yesterday, I cooked it up with a piece of willow bark and drank the soup, and last night I slept very well.' (*The Courage of the Emperors*, vol. 1)

Or again: 'The prisoners were driven by hunger to eat flesh taken from human corpses' (*My Homeland and the Peaceful Liberation*). So isn't this just like revisiting the years when we were driven by starvation even beyond the refusal to eat the flesh of human corpses? Throughout the history of the Tibetan people, far from having to drink their own urine and eat human flesh, one cannot even find records of people starving to death. The incidence of such total horrors in recent history is the accomplishment of those who claim always to be 'serving the people'.

The punishment ground in hell

Up to now, famous, knowledgeable, capable, courageous, brave and farsighted Tibetans have been falsely accused by the dictators and punished with deprivation of freedom. For example, the 10th Panchen Lama expressed limitless praise and flattery for them, saying things like: 'In the case of our own Tibet region, we are on the point of transforming from the old society to the new, from darkness to bright light, from suffering to happiness, from exploitation to equality, and from poverty to progress, and have started on a new and brilliant era in our history' (70,000 Character Petition), but even he was locked away for almost a decade.[19] Likewise, no end of able individuals were unfairly sentenced and imprisoned, and in this year's peaceful revolution too, more than 200 people have been sentenced so far, as can be seen from unofficial reports published on the internet.[20] Since this was simply for breaking laws passed by the dictators with the sole intention of preserving their hold on power, it is only the continuation of their practice of legal prosecution in violation of morality and principle. From time to time, autocratic régimes pass various legal edicts designed to consolidate their hold on power that violate universal values, and these edicts that they hold to be vital are precisely edicts from hell for those who favour freedom, equality and democracy.

While subjecting those detained in the course of the peaceful revolution to brutal discipline and terrifying intimidation, they were interrogated about which organisation they belonged to, what was their plan, who supported them, who were their collaborators; and when these investigations proved fruitless, innocent people were and continue to be charged under whichever provisions from the relevant edicts from hell, and prosecuted in secret. From start to finish, their crimes were given as nothing other than: 'Seeking to split the country', 'Seeking to overthrow state authority', 'Leaking state secrets' and so on. They are ever sensitive to anything concerning 'the state' and 'state authority', regarding it as vital, and whoever they decide has jeopardised 'the state' or 'state authority' is punished with anything from several years in prison to execution.

This is supposed to be like the saying 'If the head is tied down, the body will tremble' (with fear). The dictators always and in all respects conflate the particular interests of their faction with those of 'the state' and 'state authority', and constantly use these terms to enforce their power over the people. For them, this year's peaceful revolution was 'not about nationality issues or religious issues or human rights issues, but about the issue of state authority'. Anyone they charge with opposing a basic principle of their rule, such as 'state authority', becomes what we would call a 'political prisoner'. The given charge of 'endangering the state and state authority' really means that the accused is suspected of posing a threat to the power of the dictators.

In a totalitarian state, there are many examples of crimes that would never be considered as such in the rest of the world, like the political offences for which five-year-old children and 81-year-old seniors have been imprisoned. A few years ago, the five-year-old 11th Panchen Lama was put under house arrest,[21] and during this year's peaceful revolution, the 81-year-old printer of religious books, Peljor Norbu, was sentenced to seven years in prison. Never mind robbing the youth, who have just begun to experience life's joys and sorrows, of their liberty, where else would one see a judicial process so barbaric as to insist on prosecuting an 81-year-old, in violation of all moral, natural and humane norms, but under a totalitarian régime? The youngest political prisoner in the world is to be found in Tibet, and the oldest. It is because the Tibetan people are human cattle that they have to bear the burden of such imprisonment, and it is because Tibetan heads are made of stone that they must be labelled with false accusations.

The terrifying battlefield

Since the peaceful revolution broke out, central hubs and junctions have all been turned into firing ranges, guns and artillery put in place, an atmosphere to make your hair bristle. Towns and monasteries are patrolled by police and filled with informers; there is fear and terror, snipers lie concealed on rooftops and on street corners, spies lie in wait, enough to make your flesh crawl and your bones shiver. Anyone going to town or visiting a monastery is searched, questioned and registered at gunpoint, enough to make you shake and tremble. Monks are mostly forced back to the villages, villagers mostly confined in their homes, telephone lines and internet, tea shops and eating houses are all watched and listened to, whether near or far, all have been reduced to paralysis and desperation. By day they prowl like jackals and wolves, by night they move stealthily like thieves, staging sudden raids on monasteries and households, searching them from top to bottom and bottom to top for photos of the Dalai Lama, for hidden weapons, and for cash and valuables while they are at it, throwing Lama photos on the floor and treading on them. They call Him a 'beast with a human face', and a 'wolf in monk's robes'. They show the signs of both intoxication and planetary affliction[22] (for Red Army soldiers with heads but no brains, tanked up on the firewater of 'Motherland' and 'Great China', this is hardly surprising). When they see the implements of the Dharmapala in the protector chapels and get hold of them, they say it is evidence of hidden weapons.[23] They show all the signs of idiocy and stupidity, even persisting with far-fetched allegations they know to be wrong. They take valuables and non-valuables too, even taking half-cooked Momos[24] from the saucepan and eating them like a gang of bandits and thieves working together.

So it is that no Tibetan any longer has the right to take a hotel room in Chinese cities, and at airports they are greeted with the order to remove their hats and shoes. They are not given tickets and their money is not taken. Under the influence of deceptive propaganda, Tibetans are seen with a mixture of fear and loathing, and everyone is in a state of cautious suspicion. In short, Tibetans as a whole are seen as terrorists,[25] and under such pressure, this includes even children too young to understand.

In fact, this is by no means the first time that Tibet was turned into a terrifying battlefield, for ever since coming under the rule of the dictatorship, the beatings, struggles, arrests, detentions, punishments and executions that accompanied each successive political campaign made people incapable of movement, speech or thought, and out of constant fear, everyone became like walking corpses. This is what happened fifty years ago, through the most inhumane means, as can be seen from the following accounts, like scenes from a film:

> More than ten days later, the whole valley was covered with the corpses of men and horses killed in the fighting at Kyépur Nakdzup,[26] and the orphaned children and elderly unable to move elsewhere, and there were many fearsome sights to be seen, the writhing of the wounded among the dead, the babes still sucking at the breasts of their dead mothers. (from Jamdo Rinsang's *My Homeland and the Peaceful Liberation*)

Those labelled 'rebels' being driven to hellish prisons were treated worse than animals, as related by Tibetans incapable of making such things up: 'next day we were tied suspended from the high beams across the back of the truck, so our feet did not touch the ground, and taken like that as far as Chabcha'; and 'We were taken through Trika. On the way to Trika, three people in our truck died. When the truck was moving fast, the corpses were thrown to the ground off the back of the truck' (from Jamdo Rinsang's *Listening to my Homeland*).

Of the imprisoned, those driven to their deaths by abuse, beatings and starvation were innumerable, and the way they were tortured and terrorised can be seen from the following: 'There were many prisoners whose limbs became paralysed, their legs folded at the hips and arms folded on their chests. They were told that they had to straighten their limbs, the soldiers tied ropes around their arms and legs to pull them apart, and many died from the pain' (from Jamdo Rinsang's *My Homeland and the Peaceful Liberation*).

One old woman said: 'Shot in the right thigh [considered a centre of vitality] am I, get up and go on I cannot, but though they carry me away on a stretcher, fight I did!' and that fight goes on until the 'stench of the fallen' of Tséring Dondrup's *Raging Red Wind*. 'Aku Kalden-tsang wanted to take back the bones of his dead mother and asked for them. The Peoples [Liberation] Army soldiers told him "If we put your mother's bones in Aku Tsang's mouth, will you want to eat them? What do you want to keep them for?", and beat him up.'[27]

They showed an utterly inhumane and appalling cruelty, difficult to hear about, much less witness, such that the sky itself can barely encompass. In prison:

> the Lamas were made to carry the corpses of dead prisoners, which they dumped in a ravine a little way off. The way they dumped those bodies was like the way they compress garbage in big cities today. Then that ravine became almost completely filled. They were stacked one on top of another. An average of four people were dying in each work team every day. There were 20 work teams. One day when the ravine was almost full, a kind of bulldozer came and dug some earth, and completely buried the piles of corpses. The cavity left by the digging was also a kind of

> ravine, and they dumped corpses in there too, but it filled up after two or three days. Then they dug another, on the near side. That filled up too. I know for sure that there were 15 or more of those ravines. There must have been at least 250 bodies in each of them.[28]

Nothing could be worse than this, but take the question of weapons: the international community has managed to ban, on humanitarian grounds, the use of certain kinds of weapons in warfare by treaty agreements, such as the Dum-dum bullet and chemical weapons.[29] Yet the national army of the autocratic régime has used and tested such weapons in Tibet, which it turned into a terrifying battlefield, as we see from this: [speaking of bullets fired at civilians] during the so-called 'uprising' [1958], 'if you pressed on the wound left by those bullets, there was nothing more than a slight depression, as they tore clean through the body and came out the other side'.[30] 'One time, whether because of starvation, or because of a cloud of chemical vapour I am not sure, the senses and perceptions of men and cattle became dulled. Some said it was poison gas used in warfare.'[31] If they even used internationally banned bullets and toxic weapons, who will deny that they turned, and continue to turn, Tibet into a terrifying battlefield?

From the above, we can see that there is no greater terrorist than the totalitarian régime. What is terrorism other than forcing and suppressing people, deluding and stupefying them, inflicting pain, contempt and torment with cruel and merciless intent, all the while keeping them in fear of their lives? Whatever is there in totalitarianism is also there in terrorism. In particular, the terrorism of sealing down the bodies of the common Tibetan people, sealing up the mouths of the eminent ones, and sealing off the minds of the unthinking population, and the methods of state terrorism are something they have been practising for the last half century, so who can deny that it is their basic character? If the despicable hypocrisy of handing out a brick of tea, a sack of flour and a few red Yuan [cash notes] to the poor as 'Aid' for public display did not buy off the Tibetans' incipient sense of warrior-like courage and rock-hard solidarity in the past, how will it do so now?

In brief, there are two reasons for my feeling sad: the first is that up to now the Tibetans have not developed universal conviction with respect to the universal values of freedom, equality, democracy and so on; and without the acculturated view, way of thinking, consciousness and practical application which are the roots, the foundation and the condition for such values, they will have only the view of the Buddhas and Bodhisattvas, not the view of living in this world; they will have only the thought of all sentient beings, not of one's own people and lineage; they will have only the consciousness of the cosmic realm, not of one's own land and territory; they will have only the practice of seeking refuge and prostrating themselves before the enlightened ones, not of achieving freedom and equality; they will have only the sense of royal authority, not the sense of rights and their value; they will have only inclination towards the divine and spirit worlds, and not for the human, secular realm. Having all of these haves has meant not having all the not-haves, and as these haves and not-haves came to exclude each other, so we had to suffer such consequences as these.

Second, the Karmic outcome of this was that the totalitarians turned Tibet into the lord of death's slaughterhouse, a hellish prison, a punishment ground in hell and a terrifying battlefield following the principle of one-party rule, the way of suppressing the individual and civil society, the policy of restricting public expression and deluding the masses, the particularity of holding power by force, the extreme of eliminating distinct peoples and so forth, not just now but for over half a century.

> What do I have left? Not even the right to live a simple life in freedom... Watching out for who they want to kill, who they want to arrest/Doing

whatever they want with us, we who are without freedom... There is no way our lives will be spared... We who are without the slightest freedom or equality/That is how the Tibetans languishing in jail are called.

These are the words of the young poet Yung Lhundrup: 'I consider myself a singer who puts the Tibetan peoples' feelings into song', who passed away, leaving behind many 'laments of inestimable value' like 'Freedom, oh freedom that is sought/You are watching over us, come what may...', taken from his *Tibetans Languishing in Jail*.[32]

The whole of Tibet turned into a prison, the brutality of massacres to eliminate whole populations; the torment of imprisonment survived by less than 10 per cent ('Of about 1,000 children and 600 elders, apart from a few children with parents and elders taken [by relatives], there were now 50 odd children left in the three work teams, and over ten elders. The rest had all died within half a year, or to be precise, within two or three months.' From Naktsang Nulo's *Fortunes of a Naktsang Kid*);[33] the yoke of an unjust and immoral legal system; the agony of hungry ghosts reduced to eating human waste and human flesh; the continuation of such hellish horrors into the present, are all a cause for terrible sadness.

3

FEAR OF EXTREMISM ON ALL SIDES

Thus, after many centuries of 'listening, reflecting and meditating', and 'teaching, debating and composing' on the Buddhas and Bodhisattvas, all sentient beings, the universe in its entirety, taking refuge and bowing down, the emperor supreme, emptiness and non-self, loving kindness and compassion, the divine Dharma and the spirit world etc., if we open the eye of worldly vision, like suddenly waking up, we see the 'sheep's throat' of our land broken into pieces, the 'golden hammer' of our territory crushed under heel, our race exhausted and going down. Fortunately, now that our awareness of our rights and territory has begun to emerge, and especially by gaining a sense of ourselves as a people and of our cause, we are equipped to take charge of ourselves.

In today's world, the number of sovereign nations is ever-increasing due to the growing awareness that the universal values of human rights surpass the interests of states, and the understanding that any people deserves its own territory, rights and identity. For distinct peoples to become sovereign nations has been established as a natural right in this world. Just as it is inevitable that the autocracies of this world must come around to democracy, so the democratic system is the only acceptable basis for resolving nationality issues. In my view, there are two reasons for this: one is the international principles, resolutions, declarations and treaties that most of the world's nations have signed, agreeing the right of peoples to self-determination; and the other is the resolution of nationality issues in democratic states or by democratic governments following the principle of self-determination.

Concerning the first, the concept of self-determination is considered to originate from the ideas that 'All men are born equal', that 'The rights of man are granted by heaven', that 'Power belongs to the people', and so on, and is dependent upon the efforts of its advocates in promoting its understanding. It is through the influence of these noble ideas that freedom, equality, human rights etc. for everyone have become basic principles and practices in human societies, and have brought them, and continue to bring them, to a state of freedom and well-being. The right of peoples to self-determination is one of the basic human rights, like the rights to life, to individual freedom, to property, to equal status, to assistance, to equality, to development etc., as well as an aspect of the democratic polity. Point 55 of the United Nations Charter (26 June 1945) reads: 'on the basis of respect for the principles of the peoples' right to equality and self-determination'; point 73 reads: 'each territory and its people shall develop autonomously, each under its own political system, with respect to its particular circumstances and rate of evolution'; and point 76: 'any self-governing or independent nation must promote the development of social progress'.

The Declaration on Granting Independence to Colonial Nations and Peoples (14 December 1960) says that 'All peoples have the right to self-determination. By this right, they shall freely decide their own political affairs, and pursue the development of their own economy, society and culture'; and 'By handing over all powers, in accord with the freely expressed wishes and aspirations of the peoples of those territories, with no distinction as to race, creed or skin colour, unconditionally and irrevocably, they shall enjoy full independence.'

Point five of the seven-point Declaration on the Principles of International Law (1970) concerns the 'self-determination of peoples', and in the Declaration on Permanent Sovereignty over Natural Resources (14 December 1962):

> In accord with the principle of complete equality among nations, and with mutual respect, each people and group shall freely exercise sovereignty over the natural resources pertaining to them, and are called upon to use them beneficially'; and 'the violation of the rights of peoples and communities to control their natural resources in whatever form goes against the spirit and the provisions of the United Nations Charter, is an obstacle to the development of international cooperation, and to the maintenance of peace.

The first point in part one of the International Covenant on Civil and Political Rights (16 December 1966) reads: 'All peoples have the right to self-determination. With this right, they shall freely decide their own political affairs, and work freely towards the development of their economy, society and culture'; and: 'In accord with the fixed conditions of the UN Charter, we call for the realisation of self-determination, and affirm such rights.' The first point in part one of the International Covenant on Economic, Social and Cultural Rights (1966) repeats the same language, as does the Resolution on the Right of Peoples and Nations to Self-Determination (1952): 'With the right to self-determination, peoples and nations have finally been guaranteed all the basic human rights.' (The UN Charter, resolutions, declarations, conventions etc. are only legal principles, not laws.)

Concerning the second reason, democratically governed regions and states treat the rights of distinct peoples living in their territory in accord with the spirit and provisions of self-determination of peoples and nations in the UN Charter, resolutions, declarations and conventions as mentioned above, like the state of Montenegro, which won independence through democratic elections in 2006. This is a case of resolution achieved in accord with the human and nationality rights envisaged by the UN Charter and other such documents; there is also the case of Kosovo, which gained independence through democratic elections in 2008, with the Albanian nationality being accorded the human and nationality rights envisaged there. Similarly, there are quite a few nationalities enjoying political autonomy under democratic systems that guarantee their rights, like the French island of Corsica, where 80 per cent of residents voted in a referendum to remain under French sovereignty. In 1921, after Britain consented to Irish independence, the British and Irish sides agreed a treaty giving the people of Northern Ireland the right of self-determination to decide whether to join the Irish Republic or remain part of the United Kingdom, and eventually they chose the latter. There are also the examples of the Basques, who gained the right of autonomy from Spain in the 1970s, and the Quebecois, who gained autonomy from Canada in the 1980s, on the basis of the democratic right of peoples to self-determination.

In this way, democratic states and governments enact the rights of peoples and ethnic groups by democratic and peaceful means, and those who enjoy freedom and democracy abide by, respect and defer to the provisions for human rights and the rights of peoples and ethnic groups defined in the legal documents and treaties to which they are signatories. On the principle that universal values are not to be ignored, power holders may abstain from force and intimidation even when they do not assent, as happened recently when Kosovo declared independence from the Serbian Republic, and the Serbian government replied, 'The government of Serbia in no way accepts Kosovan sovereignty ... but will certainly not use force to prevent Kosovan independence.'[1]

Fear of the political intolerance of autocratic states

The totalitarians may have signed up to documents recognising human rights, the rights of peoples and ethnic groups (the Chinese government is a signatory to most of the above-mentioned UN Conventions, including the 2004 amendment to the Charter that 'States shall respect and guarantee human rights'), but do not abide by them, abrogating and ignoring them, stamping on human and other rights, as we well know. Respect or contempt for the wishes of peoples, ethnic groups and individuals is in all respects the main difference between autocracy and democracy; and in our times, I believe there is no more important condition than this determining whether humankind achieves peace and happiness. For instance, if one has to live in the same house as a relative who is narrow-minded, old-fashioned and obstinate, violent and cruel, whose greed leaps like a tiger, who pursues his own interests as stealthily as a wolf, whose malevolence is as fierce as a wild yak, who doggedly holds grudges, is as attached to self-gratification as a pig, crafty as a fox, oblivious of moral consequences, without shame or restraint, and who does not keep his word, even if he does share the same religion and culture, is there any way to live 'harmoniously' with such a relative?

Rather, since there is an ancient precedent that 'The Tibetans shall live peacefully in Tibet, and the Chinese shall live peacefully in China',[2] and even by today's standards, Tibet evidently meets the conditions for statehood implied by the Montevideo Convention on the Rights and Responsibilities of States: 1) a settled population 2) a distinct territory 3) with its own government and 4) capable of conducting genuine relations with other states, a revolution inspired by the unpopularity of the autocratic régime was just waiting to happen.

That is why, in the uprising for our freedom and rights in this year's peaceful revolution, because of the constant, heavy suppression, coercion and agony, incidents of 'beating, smashing, looting and burning' took place as a matter of fact. The instigators, those who lit the fuse of this year's beating, smashing, looting and burning, were, just as in the so-called 'Lhasa disturbances' of 1989, none other than the dictators themselves. We may not so far have seen any leaked internal documents showing that it was produced by the deliberate policy or gross distortions of the régime, but all kinds of indications recorded by the foreign media provide reliable evidence that the culpable instigators who indulged in destruction and blackened the innocent out of malice were, as in the past, the dictators themselves.

As Te'urang wrote in *Written in Blood*, the confirmation provided by four main witnesses is there to see,[3] but given the dictatorship's long-established practice of making deception a fine art and falsification a matter of course, they are oblivious, no matter how much careful analysis and proof one presents. No matter how much one seeks to establish black and white or distinguish true from false, the only witness to the battles of tigers and leopards in the shady depths of the forest is the blue sky above, and no amount of investigation can get to the core. So, having talked it over and thought it through, and because Tibetans know the psychology of other Tibetans, to be perfectly honest, I can infer that the protesters were led into misbehaviour by the influence of the crowd, by panic of the moment, and imitated those indulging in violence without thinking. This shows, I think, that there was nothing more than unplanned incidents with no particular aim. By comparison with the systematic, organised, intentional, long-term beating, smashing, looting and burning by the dictatorship, any little incident does not amount to a hundredth, a thousandth or a ten thousandth, as everyone well knows. That is the difference between large-scale beating, smashing, looting and burning, and small-scale.

It is a fact that situations of beating, smashing, looting and burning occurred in the course of this year's peaceful revolution, and we must own up to it. But that was small-scale. There are two reasons for saying so: one is that people were panicked and led into imitative behaviour; the other is that it was not organised or planned. Beating people, smashing things, looting property and burning goods is by definition violent activity. Both large and small instances of beating, smashing, looting and burning are violent in form and intimidatory in nature. For me, violent and intimidatory behaviour is absolutely not something to be encouraged or spread. I do not approve of beating, smashing, looting and burning whether large or small. It goes without saying that this year's revolution was a peaceful one, and everyone knows that it is inappropriate for a peaceful revolution to be characterised by violent activity. It is hard to advance one's cause through small-scale beating, smashing, looting and burning, but it cannot match up to large-scale beating, smashing, looting and burning any more than an egg can break a rock.

What then is large-scale beating, smashing, looting and burning? There were fifty years during which Tibetans, from Lamas and chieftains through aristocrats and nobles to ordinary people, men and women, young and old, from farmers and nomads to blacksmiths and cobblers, in their thousands, tens and hundreds of thousands, regardless of status, property, education or ability, willingness to fight or culpability, were beaten, whipped, clapped in irons, shot, imprisoned, 'struggled' and starved to death. Even now, they refuse to renounce this way of doing things, and the systematic and deliberate 'suppression of the big, squeezing of the small, hammering down those who stick out, and beating everyone flat' is, after all, a big beating, as any Tibetan knows.

The systematic and deliberate smashing of people's heads, of a people's will, of a sovereign territory, of its natural treasury, of the contents of monasteries, of the property of civilians, of their political identity, the roots of their prosperity and the fabric of their culture was after all a big smashing, on a scale rarely seen in this world.

When you deprive a people of the right to self-determination, you deprive them of the rights to life, to property, to equal status, to aid, to equality, to personal liberty, to expression, to religious belief, to free assembly, to the right not to suffer absolute poverty, and not to live in fear, and when this is done systematically and deliberately, it is, after all, a big loot, as anyone but a sheep would know.

Then, systematically and deliberately burning what grows above ground, burning the treasures buried underground, burning the inheritance of the elders, and especially burning people's minds is, after all, a big burn-up, that has made everyone helpless and desperate.

Beating, smashing, looting and burning. Tibetans don't know how to apply this label, or if they do know, they cannot say so, out of fear. I would say that this label with which they have been accused applies to nothing better than the deliberate, systematic and enduring policies of the régime, which are beating, smashing, looting and burning writ large.

In a situation where all feel helpless and desperate, the outbreak of small-scale beating, smashing, looting and burning is not without reason. There cannot be many instances in this world of the past and ongoing infliction of large-scale beating, smashing, looting and burning on such a meek and tame people. I do not speak as someone who has undergone the suffering of large-scale beating, smashing, looting and burning myself, but as a member of a people that has, and continues to suffer it, hearing about it and thinking about it, it makes me shiver, and that is the first of my fears, fear of the political wrath of the dictators.

FEAR OF EXTREMISM ON ALL SIDES

Fear of extreme nationalism

Unless the Sino-Tibetan issue, or to put it more precisely, the issue between the Tibetans and the autocratic régime, is resolved now—by resort to freedom, equality and democracy—to the earlier status of 'Tibetans living peacefully in Tibet and Chinese living peacefully in China', they will continue to dominate, using the theory and practice of beating, smashing, looting and burning, systematically and deliberately, to wipe out 'within fifteen years' the people of 'the last untouched land'[4] with even more pollution of the natural environment, plundering of natural resources, population transfer and political repression. In this scenario, one can foresee a long-term pattern of interaction leading to the transformation of this peaceful trans-Himalayan realm into a new battlefield in a world of perpetual bloodshed.

On one side, the Tibetans starting to gain a sense of their identity have none of the well-oiled military force, the cracking armoury and weaponry, the stocks of poison gas and explosives of the dictatorship that rules them, but they have the weapons of courage and faith in plenty, and are well-armoured with the powers of forbearance and dedication. They are starting to develop consciousness of their statehood, sovereignty; political, territorial, national and human identities; awareness of freedom, equality, rights, selfhood and democracy, and an opposition to autocratic domination, deceit and hypocrisy, coercion and repression; to beating, smashing, looting and burning. They are flush with the courage to endure hardship and suffering for the sake of universal values, without regard for personal gain, repute, comfort or praise, and even to give up their own lives without hesitation. They are mainly influenced by the outlook of loving kindness and compassion, and Bodhicitta, but they have the faith of last resort, that for the sake of the teachings and the teachers, the violent elimination of any 'enemies of the faith' and 'heretics' will not lead one to hell. The old saying that 'Tibetans are undone by hope' should now be changed to 'Tibetans are strengthened by hope'.[5] Such are the Tibetan people, unafraid and determined that 'it is better to die defiant as a tiger' for what one wants.

On the other side stand the keenly nationalistic Chinese, the autocratic government backed by a million-strong army, police and armed security forces, convinced of its own superiority, tense and headstrong, with its flagrantly aggressive policy of domination by force, possessed by the mentality of violent struggle that says 'Power comes from the barrel of the gun', and the credo of dictatorship that 'A lie repeated a hundred times becomes the truth'.[6] Apart from occasionally pumping up its own people and feeding them insidious ideas to inflame nationalist sentiment in order to shore up and defuse threats to its own power, it keeps the majority of Chinese people in suspended animation, with their heads in the clouds and their feet not touching the ground.

There was a time when they used to greet each other by asking 'Have you eaten?' in the same way that Tibetans greet each other with a 'How are you?' or '*Tashi Delek!*', from which one readily sees that earlier generations had lived through extreme hunger. But since 'Reform and Opening Up', and entering a period in which people are moderately better off and there is no shortage of foodstuffs, there are many given to boasting that in fifty years the Chinese people will be masters of the planet and China will rule the world. In particular, following this year's peaceful revolution they staged a series of incidents and demonstrations at home and abroad as a show of force bearing all the signs of extreme nationalism, and we saw and heard many things like 'All Tibetans should be killed, thrown out, eliminated!' This is proof of the saying that 'No hat will fit a beggar who has gone up in the world', the arrogance and self-importance of a people prepared to ignore truth and reality in a time of affluence, as can be seen from the postings on Woeser's 'Invisible Tibet' blog:[7]

> The fact is that nationality issues are basically decided by force of numbers, and the best solution to the Tibet issue is population transfer.
>
> One: Since the methods used in Xinjiang have brought results, the central government should think about setting up a 'Tibet Production and Construction Corps'. If they can subdue a wild people like the Uighurs, how will a people like the Tibetans be able to fight back?
>
> Two: Since the Han are in any case the dominant nationality, they are somewhat restrained in cracking down on Tibetans out of bad conscience, but the Hui people[8] don't think that way, so the Hui of Ningxia should be encouraged to migrate to Tibet, sent to dilute the Tibetan population, and to build lots of mosques, using one enemy to subdue another, for we should not hesitate to play dirty if it is in the national interest.
>
> Three: Limit the increase of the Tibetan population through birth control.
>
> Four: To celebrate the union of Chinese and Tibetans and to guarantee the assimilation of nationalities, since the population of the Tibetan autonomous prefectures in Kham and Amdo (Chinese: Qing Chuan Gan) adds up to the population of a single city they should just be designated as a city, and 'autonomous prefectures' and 'autonomous regions' will automatically disappear.
>
> Five: Suppression ought to be brutal, and mercy is inappropriate. China is a nuclear power, and we don't care whatever the West might say. China is not Serbia. Even if it wants to wipe out one of its nationalities, no one can do anything about it. Indeed, China is already accused of genocide, and the Dalai[9] proclaims everywhere that China killed more than a million Tibetans. China should kill more of them, then we would not think the accusation of 1.2 million dead so grave.

From this, one can see that there is a half-serious conspiracy among many Chinese; but in any case, on the other side, there are the Chinese people, who take aggressive nationalism to the extreme with no regard for the rest of the world.

These two peoples are distinct peoples who have fought in the past, gained victories and suffered defeats at each other's hands.

No doubt, the 'reward of fighting' for the last fifty years has been defeat for the Tibetans, but going back to the imperial period, we find the Tibetans conquering even the capital of China.[10] This time, if it is to be fought out through violent confrontation according to the logic of dictatorship, it may not be a question of coming to blows with fists and guns, and Tibetans may be outnumbered 200 to one, but if they come to be guided by an attitude of revenge and returning poison for poison, there is no saying that each Tibetan will not be reborn like Gar Tri Tring.[11] If that happens, they may not fight back like tigers and leopards, but they could fight like dogs and wolves, and 'if men have no sausage to eat, and dogs no sausage broth', it is not impossible that this Tibet will become a field of all-out battle.

However, the present revolution and advocacy of freedom and democracy are peaceful, and since the progress of peaceful revolution and peaceful advocacy cannot depend on strength of arms or numbers of people, it is difficult to say who is winning or losing. In any case, my fear is that if these two peoples take nationalism to extremes, there is a grave danger of getting locked into violent confrontation, and there is no guarantee that they will not become state terrorists on one side and nationalist terrorists on the other. So as a pacifist, thinking on this, reflecting and weighing things up, my second fear is the danger of either the state or its citizens falling into extreme nationalism.

Fear for my own wellbeing

When at leisure to do so, I have stated that 'Freedom is a hundred and a thousand times more valuable than my own life, and I will fight for it', with as much bravado as you please; yet this year, when Tibetans were staging a peaceful revolution for the sake of freedom, I shrivelled up, saying and doing nothing, and acting unconcerned. This was not out of stupidity, perversity or cunning, nor was it an outward display of integrity or discretion. It was because, one, I was quite unprepared; two, I was scared for myself; three, I was worried about what I stood to lose, and ultimately I was in fear for my own personal wellbeing.

One: to be honest, as far as I was concerned, this year's large-scale revolution was something I had never even dreamed of and that came without warning. Hitherto, I was resigned to the assumption that, as I wrote:

> apart from a small group of courageous individuals, the majority do not know the meaning of freedom and equality, whether it is something to eat or to drink. They think that if they are not going hungry or their backs are not cold, they have freedom and equality. Even if they have heard talk of such things, they think that it is something they can never get, unless the gods, or the Buddhas, or some king or lord presents it to them, and putting their faith in whichever high Lama, they remain idle.

I thought the Tibetans were far from the awareness of freedom. Thinking that it was important to plant the seed of the awareness of freedom from the vantage of advanced education and high thinking, I raised political issues as well as I knew how, but when the Tibetan people came out of nowhere on an active quest for freedom, rights and democracy, it left me astounded.

We are always going on about awareness, about courage, but for it to manifest visibly and tangibly in a short time was unimaginable. Thinking about this, if one proposes, as I do here, that Tibetans staged a peaceful revolution because of a conscious awakening to freedom and democracy, rather than just in desperation with all they have to put up with, it may be hard to say how much this accords with reality; but out of conviction, my aspiration that it does is strong, so by all means, this peaceful revolution threw all my ideas into disorder and upset things in all respects. Objectively, my earlier views that Tibetans have a mean outlook and low level of awareness were completely wrong and have gone the way of all fallacies, which led me to doubt myself too. To speak with too much confidence is not just wrong but shameful, and has to be corrected with due contrition. On reflection, it's not that I didn't have cause to develop these mistaken ideas, and year after year I went into the office with the air of someone who thinks and expresses views, but was left sitting there, with nothing to go on concerning what most people think. On the other hand, in view of what I wrote in those years, Tibetans cursed me as a heretic and a heathen, and cast me out of their ranks, so it was rare for me to meet people who would share their true sentiments.[12] Because of these circumstances, I had pretty much become like a hibernating marmot, and not a word about the imminent outbreak of peaceful revolution reached my ears, so at the crucial moment I was completely unprepared and found myself unable to do anything.

Two: is fear for my own life and wellbeing. During this year's peaceful revolution, the régime used force to tie and bind Tibetans, arrest and hold them, detain and restrict them, punish and kill them, and even when I heard, saw and became aware of those they call 'Beaters, smashers, looters and burners', I kept a disciplined silence and stayed passive like a coward, ultimately out of fear. But then, watching people going through hell for real, my mouth gaping and eyes wide open, gasping *'Akha!'* (Oh no!) and *'Atsi!'* (Oh dear!), as if instantly flattened by the weight of pain and agony, I felt that there was no light in the sky, no justice on earth, that I had neither compassion for others nor strength in myself, could not eat during the day nor sleep at night, and watching the spectacle of force and intimidation played out again and again, whatever you see appears hostile, whatever you perceive is the enemy, you are angry with everything and hold grudges against everyone. I got to thinking that there could be no worse suffering than this, even if someone were to murder your own father; because for my part, every time my thoughts turn to the methods of torture used by the dictators, my hair stands on end, I get gooseflesh and my heart leaps into my throat.

> Pulling out hair and facial hair, kicking and slapping, pinching and poking, pushing and pulling, some people used big keys [the keys for old-fashioned Tibetan locks, often used as a weapon in fights] and rods to beat those subjected to 'Struggle', until blood ran from their noses and mouths and they passed out, causing severe injuries like broken limbs and so on. (70,000 Character Petition)

Punching, kicking and administered beatings are nothing, among the more excruciating punishments they have are: 'Pao Lao' (炮烙), 'riding the copper horse', or the punishment of being burned alive by riding on a flaming hot (metal) 'horse'; 'Nao Gu', putting the head in a vice and tightening it until the eyes pop out, the skull splits, and eventually the brains come out; 'Pou Fu' (剖腹), cutting open the abdomen, removing the internal organs and then pulling out the intestines; 'Rou Shua' or 'Shu Xi', 'flesh scraping', scraping the flesh off the bones with a serrated knife; 'Yao Zhan' (腰斩), the punishment of crippling by breaking the pelvis; 'Ling Chi' or 'Qian Dao Wan Gua' (千刀万剐), death by a thousand cuts; 'Che Lie' (车裂) or 'Wu Ma Fen Shi' (五马分尸), dismemberment of a person by having five horses or oxen pull the limbs and head in different directions; 'Ru Jia', 'breast squeezing', squeezing and then cutting off a woman's breasts; 'Mu Lü' (木驴), 'the wooden donkey', a pointed wooden pole is inserted into a woman's genitals, and after riding the wooden donkey she is in agony, no longer able to bend or straighten up; 'Bao Pi' (包皮), 'skinning alive', tearing off the skin from the head down and across the back; 'Ju Wu Xing' or 'Da Xie Ba Kuai', dismembering the body in five parts, the four limbs and the trunk, or in eight parts, where both eyes are gouged out and both ears cut off in addition; 'Peng Zhu' (烹煮), being cooked alive in a clay pot; 'Gong Xing' (宫刑), castration, removal of the penis and testicles; 'Yue Xing', the punishment of crippling by breaking the kneecaps; 'Zhan Cha Zhi Jia Feng', inserting iron nails under the fingernails; 'Huo Mai' (活埋), 'burying alive', being buried in the ground up to the neck; 'Zhen Du', poison; 'Zhuang Xing', driving a stake all the way into either the mouth or the anus; 'Tie Ju', drawing a line from the head down, or from the bottom up, and cutting along it with a saw; 'Duan Zhui', twisting the neck and spinal cord; 'Guan Chang', pouring molten copper or lead down the throat.

Such are the extremely cruel and hellish punishments that we have not seen but read about, that they actually used to practise, as can be seen from their history. Such punishments, that demons could scarcely conceive, much less humans, exceed by a hundred and a thousandfold the punishments used in old Tibet, like gouging out eyes, cutting out tongues, cutting off ears, cutting off limbs, breaking heels, putting hands in boiling oil, riding the copper horse, stitching up in leather sacks (and throwing into rivers), putting on the stone hat, whipping with willow branches and stinging nettles, locking up in a cage, wearing the cangue, leg irons, hanging stones around the neck, crucifixion, suffocation, crushing the chest with boulders, throwing into a pit of scorpions, binding hands in leather, castration, dismemberment, bamboo spikes (under the fingernails), administered beatings, whippings and so on. Just thinking about them even for a moment makes me tremble.

Granted, these punishments belong to the distant past and are no longer practised, but it is certainly possible that those who devised punishments that could scarcely have occurred to the human imagination, and inflicted them on anyone who happened to be found guilty, carry some kind of habitual imprint as a result. There is no trusting the kind who do not flinch from cruelties that the rest of us would be petrified just to witness, as can be seen from the invention of various electronic punishment devices in the high-tech age.

Nameless instruments of punishment do the work of striking, beating, hitting, chaining, immobilising, grabbing, binding, suppressing, squeezing, pinning down, poking, hurting, ripping and so on using the power of electricity and drugs. They require no manpower, and they are precise, thorough, powerful and effective enough to rend flesh from bone, dislocate joints and fry internal organs, all without breaking the skin. There are unquestionably all kinds of devices of punishment that can destroy the mental faculties, diminish awareness and induce delusion, without leaving wounds on the body, and we know this because sometimes those in detention are tortured to death, and the corpse is not returned to the family but cremated in secret, out of public view.

It scares me to think how my basically unwell body would cope just with deprivation of food and sleep, never mind the sufferings of the hottest and coldest hells. At that time, there is a good chance that you might ruin your name for life, disgrace yourself by weeping and wailing, and while pleading for leniency and forgiveness, mention a few names. It is terrifying to think that there is every certainty that one's determination never to become a lackey of the régime could be shaken from its foundations.

So it is that just thinking about a single aspect of the dictators' torture methods brings terrible, quaking fear. Whether this is because of my cowardice, or thinking I know all about what I have never experienced is uncertain, but fear is fear, and there may not even be an explanation for it.

Three: any apprehensions of loss can probably be included in the fear category. Any Tibetan has to take some position with regard to an important event like this, and as a Tibetan who usually likes to put both sides and likes to argue for and against, who was unable to get practically involved, I really should be ready to speak my mind in a timely way. That I was not able to do so is because I too belong to the famous vested interests in society, I am a salaried man, an ox with a hump of fat. The vested interests in society always take the small matter of personal welfare and interests very seriously, but are unconcerned with wider issues of great importance; on the contrary, they serve as an ally of the dictators. As a member of the vested interests in society, if my interests expire, I am at risk of unthinkable hardship, unable to provide for and support my aged parents before me, my children after me, and the spouse by my side, and if I were to fall into that predicament, there is no safeguard to prevent me from becoming someone else's slave for life. Since the institution of the politically highly misleading policy of 'Taking economic progress as central', myself and everyone else have been possessed by the demon of money, and especially fat hump oxen like me have turned into creatures who think of nothing else, not even counting those of limited means among the ranks of men, like the saying 'When you are well-off, everyone comes meekly in front of you; but when you are not, they will point at you with derision from afar'. The saying 'If you have means, you are your uncle's nephew; if you don't have means, you are your uncle's servant' seems to be true, for if you have nothing, there is a strong possibility that you will spend your life as someone's servant, not a prospect that I would find acceptable. And when the body is unwell, considering and coming to terms with the possibility of separation from loved ones is terrifying.

In frankly letting my thoughts be known here, I am not claiming that the heroes and heroines who joined in this year's peaceful revolution had no such fear or caution, nor asking for anyone's sympathy, nor trying to justify my silence and passivity. I am just honestly expressing my way of thinking, because whether you curse me or ridicule me or even try to find fault, that is the situation, the third of the fears, the concern for one's own life and wellbeing.

Fear for the future

There is another fear: as already mentioned, it is undeniable that incidents of what the régime branded as 'beating, smashing, looting and burning' did take place in the course of this year's peaceful revolution. I have suggested that this was because of panic and imitative behaviour and since there are irrefutable signs that such a sincere, determined and inclusive revolution will continue, that the struggle will be thoroughgoing and widespread, there is no guarantee that when revolution and conflict breaks out again, there will not be a repeat of the 'beating, smashing, looting and burning'. And if that happens, there is no doubt that the régime will resume their bloodletting and turn the place into the lord of death's slaughterhouse. Anticipating that, like knowingly smashing an egg against a rock, like the contest between a moth and the flame, makes me fearful. A fiery politician might well say that there is no gaining freedom without loss of life, that East Timor paid with a hundred thousand lives before gaining independence; but when I think about the view of freedom and democracy held by myself and others, the [low] ideological level and the political environment, and in particular, taking myself as an example, feeling paralysed with fear for family and friends, never mind my own life, in the face of torture and suffering, as described before, I have absolutely no enthusiasm for violent struggle.

The dictators have found neither a scapegoat, nor a 'towel' (to clean their hands), so if 'beating, smashing, looting and burning' or similar violence breaks out again, it will play straight into their hands. For a start, they will take pictures, film it, and make it into a video to show their own people, who know and understand nothing, as a way of shoring up support; and next, they will surely use it to justify a crackdown even more severe than before, in which many lives will be lost, more will suffer detention and torture, and even more will suffer the pain of separation from loved ones whether dead or still alive.

That may be frightening enough, but there is one scenario we really do not want to see, and that is the grave danger of Tibetans taking the path of retaliation and vengeance, out of desperation, using poison gas and explosives, and carrying out assassinations and murders like terrorists. I say with measured words: 'If you go down the path of barbarism, you have chosen the path that will lead to the total destruction not just of intangible things like religion and culture, but of things as tangible as your own homeland ringed by snowy mountains and ultimately your whole people.' I say definitively: 'If you go with violence, you will render meaningless all that our people at home and in exile have worked for up to now, and nullify the achievements of this year's great peaceful revolution. You would be knowingly following an extremist and nihilist path.'

I have two reasons for saying this: inner factors for ourselves and outer factors for others. First: Tibetans lived for a thousand years shunning politics; in all that time there was no major political disturbance, so we don't even have the experience of political conflict. This lack of experience could be seen from this year's peaceful revolution: its disorganised, unplanned and free-for-all character. In my view, the Tibetan psychology is a primitive one, in which many characteristics of pre-civilised peoples can be seen. Like thinking that the revolution has succeeded just because many people made a spontaneous show of bravado, or like some people thinking that just because they got hurt in the violence of 'beating, smashing, looting and burning', out of imitating thuggery, they had been fighting for freedom. Such activities leave nothing behind but a pile of ash, and thus have no lasting significance. This is one sign of a primitive people with no experience of political struggle.

Qualities like spontaneity and bravado are indeed indispensable to the organisation and leadership of political struggle, but since a message with no figurehead to lead it will consist of whatever comes into people's heads, organisation and leadership are most important, especially to stop the struggle turning into violent confrontation. How could a primitive people still in the clutches of an old-world psychology of demons and spirits, with no history or experience of political struggle, take on an autocratic state with generations of experience, backed by a modern army? The outcome is a foregone conclusion. Even if we suppose that the discrepancy in forces were evened out, they could never be matched in terms of trickery and deceit. So I would say that until the ground rules of the conflict change, to think about meeting aggression with retaliation is deliberately to hand them the excuse for wiping us out as a people.

Second: After the '9/11 incident' in 2001, the US government came out with a list of the world's terrorists and terrorist organisations, centred on those in Muslim countries like Palestine and Afghanistan, including Islamic Jihad, Islamic Liberation Front, Hamas, Al Qaeda, the Taleban and so on, as well as the Phillipino NPA, the Columbian FARC, the Rwandan Liberation Army, the Cambodian Khmer Rouge, the Irish Republican Army, the Nepali Maoists, the Japanese Red Army, the Aum cult, the Turkish Patriarch Party (of uncertain identity) and so on. The Uigur people in the land traditionally known as Turkestan, called 'Xinjiang' since the reign of the Qing emperor Qianlong,[13] had various organisations in exile, like the East Turkestan Islamic Movement, East Turkestan Liberation Organisation, East Turkestan Information Centre and World Uygur Youth Congress, that were put on the list.

I then heard that the régime appealed for Tibetan organisations and individuals to be included in the list too. But because the Tibetans have not so far engaged in violence, they were not listed. If they had such a record, they certainly would have been listed, and if they follow the path of violence in future, they will go straight into the terrorist category. If they get stuck with that label, the likelihood is that they would be seen as a threat by governments and individuals throughout the world. So even if the régime kills Tibetan males off altogether leaving only females,[14] there will be no one to stand up for them and provide support, even though they live under one of the cruellest autocratic régimes in the world. If you go down that road, even under a democratic government, you have to pay the price of that label. Compare with the pro-independence forces in Chechnya who engaged in violence: the democratic government of Russia branded them as terrorists and squashed them, like using an axe to flatten a flea, and they continue to do so. What could be more frightening than getting into a situation like that? So thinking of ourselves, others, everyone, I am convinced that choosing the path of violence and terrorism is choosing the path of self-destruction, and the fear of that danger is my fourth one, fear for the future.

I have written of four fears: fear of contemplating the cruelty of the régime, fear of the danger of government and individuals falling into extreme nationalism, fear for one's own life and well-being, and fear for the future, and at this point, I have one more fear. I am naturally terrified at the thought that once this essay has been made public, I will eventually have to endure the hot hells and cold hells on earth. I may 'lose my head because of my mouth', but this is the path I have chosen, so the responsibility is mine.

4

A LESSON IN THE PEACEFUL WAY TO RESOLVE ALL

Now I will get on to the main subject I want to talk about, namely 'the right to civil disobedience', 'the practice of truth-insistence', 'the organisation of non-violent non-cooperation', which are different facets of the same thing, different names with the same meaning.

Initially there are two points to be explained: first, we used to translate the Chinese term 'Gong Min Bu Fu Cong' (公民不服从) (civil disobedience) into Tibetan as '*Chimang gi tsikur michépa*' (refusal to obey by the public); but thinking that this was neither easy to pronounce nor succinct in meaning, I have amended the translation to '*Chimang gi mitönpa*' (civil non-cooperation/disobedience). This is because, according to Tsenlha Ngawang Tsultrim's 'Golden Mirror' lexicon, '*Tönpa* as a suffix means 1. confidence 2. desire 3. following after, in archaic usage', and this archaic form, with the negative prefix, conveys the sense of the Chinese term. So, the '*Tönpa Shi*' (four reliances) and '*Mitönpa Shi*' (four non-reliances) are terms familiar from our religious recitations, and besides, archaic usage needs to be given a new lease of life.

I don't know how well it translates the English term 'civil disobedience', but it gives a sense of when the public does not trust unjust laws and orders imposed by a government, does not follow them, does not obey them, does not accept them, does not agree to them, does not respect them, does not honour them, does not welcome them, and expresses opposition. Not being able to think of a term more pronounceable, comprehensible and succinct, I have translated it this way. As for the 'right to civil disobedience', I have not seen this term much in the relevant sources. Anyway, these terms are new to the Tibetan language, as something not experienced, even less talked about.

Interestingly, civil disobedience has now become a subject of socio-political philosophy, with individual scholars expressing various views on it, such as whether or not it is a natural or innate obligation, whether or not it violates the norms of social behaviour, whether or not it can become a commonly accepted standard of truth among people, whether or not it can be practised under autocratic rule, whether or not it depends on the principle of self-determination in democratic politics, how the legal parameters of civil disobedience are defined, how the term 'civil' is vague and open to various interpretations and so on, and there is much current study on this. Theory always 'comes after', and while it is the place of theorists and -ologists to 'come after', I have no grasp or training in theory, and no confidence to propose analyses. My basic concern is with the need for practical application, and I will try to give an initial introduction in common-sense terms as best I can, using language appropriate to the time and place.

The right to civil disobedience

To discuss the terms 'civil', 'disobedience' and 'right', as well as 'civil disobedience', I will divide them into four.

1. *'Civil'*

'Civil' or 'citizen' refers to subjects of a state, or 'natural persons'. In this context, 'natural person' does not mean the social individual, but should be understood in the sense of the Chinese term 'Fa Ren' (法人), meaning 'legal person' or 'legal unit', a legal term very difficult to render in Tibetan. Anyone with the physical characteristics of an individual is a natural person, with an inherent entitlement to human rights. These natural persons have obligations to the state according to the criteria specified in the constitution, and entitlement to political, economic and social rights. Whichever state they belong to, natural persons or individuals may not be distinguished, discriminated against or subjected to unequal treatment due to race, skin colour, gender, language, religion or political beliefs. All are equal before the law, and according to this principle, individuals are equally entitled to the fundamental rights of freedom of migration, freedom of expression, freedom of self-determination, freedom to write and publish, freedom of private communication, freedom of religious faith, freedom of conscience, freedom of moral conduct, freedom of assembly, freedom of association, freedom to stop work, freedom to own property, freedom of movement, freedom of personal values and so on, as well as the right to participate in the government of the state, to elect and be elected to office, and to participate in policy-making. Likewise, they are obliged to follow the constitution and the law, to keep state secrets, to follow social norms, to safeguard public property, uphold public regulations and so forth, and these are the rights and obligations that define citizens. All inherent political, economic and social rights of the individual are protected by law, and individuals have the responsibility to obey all provisions of the law. The 'people' of democratic polities in which all have the right to equality before the law are thus known as citizens.

According to the connotations of the term 'citizen', it applies to democratic political systems, not to autocratic ones. 'Disobedience/non-cooperation' takes place in democratic systems, maybe because it is recognised as a right by those systems, but it is practised only in democratic societies, or in societies governed by consensual principles of justice, and is hardly found in autocratic societies. Thus, 'citizen' is a term properly applied only to democratic societies.

2. *'Disobedience'*

'Disobedience/non-cooperation' means deliberately disobeying, disregarding, refusing to follow and opposing by non-violent means the unjust law or order of a government (or other agency) imposing its rule by force.

To explain it in Tibetan terms, of the two aspects 'explanation and accomplishment', it belongs with the latter, and of the activities proper to body, speech and mind, it is in the physical category. It cannot be performed merely through listening, reflection and meditation, but requires practical action.[1] It can be expressed in numerous ways, demonstrated by a single individual or by many joining together, actively in advance or passively in consequence, by refusing to comply with the demands of the law or by engaging in what the law prohibits.

The ways of manifesting civil disobedience can be broadly summarised as three. The first is the legal way, which means appealing through legal mechanisms for unjust laws or orders to be amended, for instance, by presenting the case face to face, by issuing petitions and appeals, or by contesting their legitimacy in court, in parliament, or through government departments. The second is also legal, but slightly more vocal than the first, and involves applying the rights of citizens guaranteed by the constitution to stage demonstrations, public meetings and so on.

Third, if a government ignores or obstructs basic democratic rights, citizens go to greater lengths to call for justice to be applied, even if it means facing exclusion, imprisonment or ultimately death, using methods that generate public concern and sympathy. This involves deliberately breaking the law.

There are those who say that civil disobedience can only be practised in democratic societies because in autocratic societies there is greater danger that it will simply be stamped upon. Citizens of democratic polities do not just disobey unjust laws but apply just ones, for non-cooperation involves no taking of life, no arson or use of weapons, but is absolutely non-violent and peaceful, deliberately and tactically so, giving the authorities no pretext to crack down, and focusing on generating public sympathy, to open people's eyes to injustice, and show that truth is with the people, not the government. It is consistent with reason and justice, and stands for nothing other than that. It is peaceful action, with no sign of violence, coordinated at street level, without secrecy. The deliberate breaking of laws is not done out of heedlessness or ignorance, and only by undergoing hardships themselves do people call on others to do the same. To make these points easy to remember, I would summarise them as four qualities: essence, activity, necessity and objective. The essence is that truth is on our (the citizens') side, and we must practise forbearance and endurance to see it vindicated; the activity is opposing bad laws with non-violence in order to rectify them; the necessity is for open, street-coordinated action to maintain public sympathy; and the objective is freedom and happiness, asserting universal rights for the sake of peace. These I offer to my people for their consideration.

3. *The right to 'civil disobedience'*

After going through the meanings of 'civil' and 'disobedience', one would think the meaning of this term would be quite clear.

'Civil' refers to democratic society, in which citizens have political, economic and social rights protected by law, and likewise if they live within those laws, there would seem to be no need for them to practise disobedience. But because people have a variety of dispositions and beliefs, unjust laws and demands go against their political beliefs, moral values, religious beliefs and so forth, or to put it another way, if any requirement or prohibition enacted by law goes against individuals' sense of fairness, or if law and moral conduct come into conflict, they will take up disobedience against the government in power, seen as violating the law.

Whether or not it is legitimate for citizens to engage in disobedience is not something decided by the demands or prohibitions of law, for it is seen as a universal value, like the other natural and inherent rights granted by heaven, which cannot be taken away or exchanged. In particular, this is understood as the third of the three degrees of disobedience outlined above, 'going to greater lengths ... facing exclusion, imprisonment or ultimately death to amend an unjust law, using methods that generate public concern and sympathy ... which involve deliberately breaking the law, or going to the extreme'.

It is important to understand that by suggesting civil disobedience as a right, it has come to be seen in democratic societies as a paramount universal value, while in autocratic societies it is seen as just the opposite. With Tibetans living under an authoritarian crackdown, if asked: 'What is your most pressing need in resorting to civil disobedience?', I have only one thing in mind, and that is to be able to give people general advice.

4. *The origin of the term 'civil disobedience'*

'Civil disobedience' is a more recent name for something long practised. In terms of practice, it goes back to pre-Christian Greece, whereas the coining and popularising of the term, in addition to the practice, is no older than the nineteenth century. This demonstrates the gradual evolution of an individual practice into a collective political exercise.

The term was coined by H. D. Thoreau, and is explained with reference to his ideas. In 1848 he gave his famous speech on 'Resistance to Civil Government', which was published in 1866, four years after his death, under the title 'Civil Disobedience'. Since then the term has come into common currency, and these days it has become an established concept in political and social science. Thoreau was a writer, who lived at a time when the US government had still not managed to put an end to slavery and was involved in a military invasion of Mexico. Out of disgust with this, he adopted the overt practice of not paying tax to the government and non-cooperation with unjust laws, for which he was arrested and imprisoned, although he only had to spend one day in jail because someone paid to get him out. He was greatly displeased, nevertheless, and delivered the speech mentioned above which, although it came to only 10–20,000 words, became more famous than all his other writings, more influential and well-known, and came to be considered a milestone in the history of political thought.

Thoreau's short book introduced the saying 'That government is best which governs least', and 'Great claims are made for government, though it is at best a paltry mechanism', well-spoken words of undying relevance, whatever one's view of democracy. It affirmed that the individual is the foundation of the state, and in a democracy, the individual must be taken as central and all-important; that the power and authority of any state are derived from the individual, and that the individual must be recognised as a higher, independent bearer of rights. Only with such a view of the individual is a truly free and enlightened state possible. To prevent the welfare of the individual being subsumed, any government proceeding from the choices of individuals is fundamentally one that respects the wishes and rights of the individual. 'The progress from an absolute to a limited monarchy, and from limited monarchy to democracy is a progress towards true respect for the individual', he wrote, so that not only must governments and states respect the rights and wishes of individuals, but that should be their ultimate purpose; it was this theory of democracy that formed the basis of his thinking.

The government and state arise from the mutual interdependence of individuals. Any individual is first of all human, and second a citizen. The individual citizen is a moral agent, so that as a citizen, 'the only obligation I can accept is to do at any time what I think right'; in this context law is meaningless, and yet there is not a single government that is not based on law. Since human beings are moral agents, the law does not make them even the slightest bit more just, while by according the law undue respect, people implicate themselves in all manner of unjust consequences. The living people we see using their physical strength or mental faculties in the service of the state, for example, have from the very beginning become non-humans. Human robots like soldiers, prison guards, police, security guards and so on are never able to use their faculties of judgement and moral conscience in the proper way. They serve the state with their bodies, and legislators, politicians, lawyers, senior officials and so on serve with their brainpower, but from an ethical point of view, they would not know whether their efforts were serving the devil or the lord. These servants of the state who unswervingly follow its command can be reckoned to be of the same worth as horses or dogs, yet they are commended as the noblest of citizens. Whereas the few real heroes, patriots, martyrs, reformers in the highest sense who serve the state with their consciences are always seen as enemies, and the perceptions of ordinary people are no different. And with that in mind, how many eminent persons of sound judgement and moral conscience can we count in all of this vast country? No more than 1 per cent, at a guess.

If the government shows me no favours, I need show no concern about them. It has ever been the way of governments to content themselves with making a mess of whatever they do. It is hard to say whether a government that can go to the extreme of violence or reach extremes of inefficiency is of any use to us or is a government of slaves, so when it becomes intolerable, individuals have the right not to serve it, and indeed have the right to oppose it. Initiating the practice of non-cooperation by refusing to pay taxes, Thoreau said:

> As an individual of conscience, one who does not live by the brute force of the state and the majority, but following the way of principled disobedience, or my own way, I have quietly declared war on the state... I have not paid the poll tax for six years. If a thousand, or a hundred, or just ten, or even one honest man ceased to hold slaves, refused to be an owner of slaves or a collaborator in slavery, and went to jail for it, that would be the abolition of slavery in America. For it matters not how small the beginning may seem to be: what is once well done is done forever... If a thousand men were not to pay their tax bills this year, that would not be a violent and bloody measure, as it would be to pay them, and enable the state to commit violence and shed innocent blood. This is, in fact, the definition of a peaceable revolution, if any such is possible.

Here, I have just summarised Thoreau's 'Civil Disobedience', collated and outlined the main message, and rephrased it in my own words, reckoning it is an accurate representation of his views, adapted to the Tibetan way of thinking. There are no doubt points I didn't cover, conclusions I didn't follow through, and maybe misunderstandings, but it serves as an explanation, neither swallowing it whole with relish nor rejecting it altogether with cynicism.

Theorists say that Thoreau was a blind individualist, and his view of individual morality as more important than state and law as the lynchpin, faces many objections and refutations from among the blind legalists. The debate between blind individualists and blind legalists is a theoretical one, on which we cannot comment, and have no need to either. All we need to know is that the idea of civil disobedience was popularised by Thoreau.

As an individual commitment, civil disobedience has been a recognised phenomenon since the time of the ancient Greeks, over 2,400 years ago. It originated with the philosopher Socrates, whose life became a stake in the prolonged conflict between democrats and autocrats in ancient Greece. I cannot go into his role in depth, and a mere introduction would not suffice, so I will just briefly introduce his exposition of civil disobedience, based on the Crito chapter of the *Dialogues*, by Plato.

What happened was that the Athenians accused Socrates of 'Corrupting the youth, disrespecting the gods, and advocating another form of religion' (there were grounds for each charge, but I will not elaborate here for the sake of brevity). When the time of his execution approached, his friends discussed ways of arranging his escape, but as a great man of pure conduct and a guardian of truth dedicated to the pursuit of knowledge, he considered the reasons behind his friends' proposal, and declared, 'I do not live just for the sake of living, but for the sake of living properly.' Listening to the talk of escape, he said that if that option could be confirmed by careful analysis to be justified, he would consider it; but if not, he would not abandon the principle of truth. When his wife and children, his reputation, the money for passage and other reasons were put forward, he said that escape was a vulgar thing to do, and these could not be his criteria for assessing the question. The noble person owes his development to the well-governed society, and he is expected to live honestly, so his responsibility to obey the law must be admitted, and giving the law a personification, he then engages it in discussion.

The Law: 'Listen, Socrates. As you know, Athenian law says that any individual having reached adulthood who does not believe in the laws and political organisation of the Athenian state can pick up their belongings and move elsewhere. But in 70 years you never chose to do so, and on the contrary, spent your life enjoying the order, peace and freedom that Athens' laws provide. Thereby, you have a contractual obligation to Athenian law, and cannot just obey the law when you find it to your benefit, and break it when you do not. That would go against your long-held position, and the values of truth, morality, noble and proper conduct, and honest dealings that you preach. You would bring harm upon yourself, your friends and your country, set a precedent for people in future to become lawless and spoilt, and vindicate the witnesses produced by those who found you guilty of corrupting the youth. If you repay error with error and wrong with wrong, you will be seen in the afterlife, not to mention in the present, as a lawbreaker, and possibly treated with contempt, so does merely saving your life have any meaning? Better you do not sneak away like the fox despised by men and jumped at by dogs.'

Socrates and friends: 'Properly speaking, having found no justification for running away, I will be put to death not by any error of the law, which is respected by myself, others and everyone, but one committed by my fellows. Facing a false accusation, if I were to avoid death and counter their mistaken ideas with a mistaken escape on my part, that would not be morally correct. An ethical individual cannot meet bad with bad, overturn wrong with wrong, or counter aggression with aggression, so I submit to the death penalty', and he drank the poison and died.

On the face of it, this story seems to be concerned with the obligations of citizens rather than with civil disobedience. Yet, at the time of his impending death, rather than trying to avoid punishment, or secretly escape, or do anything immoral, Socrates' acceptance, when the 500 or more Athenian jurors wrongly passed the death sentence on him, can be seen basically as an attempt to rectify the faults of an unjust legal system. But most of all, testifying to his innocence of the charges of 'corrupting the youth and disrespecting the gods', it was an act of insistence on truth, of awakening the moral conscience of society at the cost of his life. Further, the use of non-violent methods, not returning bad for bad, misdeed for misdeed, wrong for wrong or aggression for aggression, or committing anything commensurate with a crime is an instance of disobedience in practice. As will be explained, it may be for these reasons that Western commentators have seen Socrates' death as the source of the civil disobedience tradition, but I have just made these comments as a distant observer.

Civil disobedience is also said to have its origins in the Western religious scriptures and philosophy. The New Testament of the Christian Bible says 'Christ is the way, and the truth, and the life', 'Cherish the lord Jesus Christ with your whole heart, your whole soul and your whole mind', 'Bow to Christ the lord, and render service to him, and no other', telling us to serve only God, not others. In Buddhism, one of the 'four [reliances and] non-reliances' is to 'Rely not on the person but on the religious law', and though they are of different character, the manner of explication looks very similar, and might be said to express the ideal of non-cooperation. Then Christ told his disciples, 'Do not resist evil people, and to he who strikes you on your right cheek, you should turn the left. To anyone who would sue you and take your shirt, give him your coat as well. Whoever forces you to go one mile, go with him two.' Compare this with the kind of discipline envisaged by the perfection of patience in the Six Perfections of Buddhism or the precepts on the practice of non-violence, with the same theme as principled disobedience, and you will see that they could have been inspired by the scriptures.

Likewise, 'non-cooperation' means not cooperating with a law of some kind, for if it is customary for people in the course of social interaction voluntarily to abide by written laws, there is also a custom of abiding by one's individual conscience, or natural law. Both formal law and natural law function to ensure proper regulation and decent behaviour in society. It is said that formal law is necessary to protect people's natural or inherent rights, like the seal guaranteeing justice. Now basically in the work of those who study political phenomena, political scientists and philosophers, all kinds of opinions have emerged: as the Greek philosopher Aristotle said,[2] 'An unjust law is no law at all', arguing that law must abide by truth. The Roman philosopher and statesman Cicero said, 'As to the profundity of the law, it may be regarded as perfect in discrimination, but to be one with the natural way of things, it would have to be followed by humanity universally and to last for all eternity.'[3] While affirming that all of us, from highest to lowest, have an obligation to obey the law, he implied that individuals should therefore not obey unjust laws, or laws that did not guarantee natural rights.

The English philosopher John Locke wrote, 'Whenever the legislators endeavour to take away, and to destroy the peoples' property, or to reduce them to slavery under arbitrary power, they put themselves into a state of war with the people, who are thereupon absolved from any further obedience',[4] which shows that the word (dis)obedience was so used. Major arguments are joined on the subject of the obedience and disobedience of citizens in the works of the philosophers Thomas Hobbes and David Hume; and the importance of the relation between the subjective individual and the objective state was emphasised by philosophers from Plato in ancient Greece to more recent sources like the Germans Georg Wilhelm Friedrich Hegel and Karl Marx. There are many views on the subject of obedience and disobedience in their works too.

As a result, civil disobedience as a political phenomenon is considered by Westerners as a part of the activist political tradition in which theory and practice are inseparable, and the commentators and analysts writing about this are many. For my part, despite my limited knowledge, I have just given a brief and easily comprehensible introduction to the emergence of civil disobedience in earlier and later times as a form of collective political action and as an individual action, with a theoretical and practical background from their religious scriptures and philosophy, one restricted by my own understanding, like the proverbial finger pointing at a mountain.

Satyagraha, or 'truth-insistence'

'Truth-insistence' is the Gandhian approach, a unique form of political action that arose during the course of the Indian Nationalist movement at the start of the twentieth century and the struggle for rights against the British rulers. Today it is known as 'the doctrine of non-violent resistance', or as 'Gandhianism', and is considered a variety of socio-political philosophy, called the philosophy of truth-insistence (or non-violent resistance).

I suppose that it is considered a type of socio-political philosophy because it has a social application, it is a form of political analysis, and it involves philosophical issues. While individuals belong each to their own countries, having a certain culture, customs and conventions in common, it has application to any society, or all human societies. As a way to get members of society to abide by law and custom, or as a common strategy for individuals or groups to advance their interests collectively, it is a political analysis; and as a philosophical argument about how people live in the world and its objective nature, it belongs to philosophical enquiry.

This socio-political philosophy bearing the seal of religious values and the hallmark of ethical conduct became a sort of profound instruction for resolving all differences, disturbances, confrontation and fighting between individuals, groups and peoples in a peaceful and non-violent way. Not only was it a panacea of guidance for the Indian independence struggle of the time, but also for successive struggles for political rights and revolutions, in countries with democracy and without, at various times, for example from the USA and Chile on the American continent, to the former Czechoslovakia, Poland and Ukraine in Europe, to South Africa on the African continent, to Burma and Kyrgyzstan in Asia—all seem to have been profoundly influenced by the doctrine of truth-insistence—and these days it has become the unique method of political struggle worldwide.

I will introduce Gandhi's truth-insistence approach under four headings:

1. *The meaning of the words*

a. 'Satyagraha' is the philosophy that inspired the political campaigns of Mohandas Karamchand Gandhi, leader of the Indian Nationalist movement and leader of the Indian National Congress, known to Indians as 'Bapu', 'father of the nation', and to Tibetans as 'Changchub Sempa' (Bodhisattva) or 'Daknyi Chenpo' (Mahatma).

   The word is in Gandhi's native Gujarati,[5] and was apparently devised in consultation with a learned person, to emphasise the noble character of Gandhi's approach and to preclude the danger of political struggle degenerating into direct confrontation.

   'Satyagraha' has been translated into English as 'truth power', 'strength of mind' or 'willpower', 'the way of truth', 'the pursuit of truth' etc. The Chinese word 'Fei Bao Li' (non-violence) (非暴力) translates only the second of its two aspects, theory and practice. It is translated into Tibetan as '*Denpé Utsuk*' (truth-insistence). 'Satya' means 'truth', and 'Graha' means 'to seize', 'to perpetuate', 'insistence', and the term is composed of these six consonants [in Tibetan transliteration]. 'Satya' represents the theoretical aspect and 'Graha' the practical aspect, and the Tibetan term does capture this adequately; but one might object that, for one thing, 'insistence' could be understood in some parts of Tibet as stubborn behaviour with no particular truth or justification, and might lead to confusion; and for another, it is not clear to me why the genitive particle was used to join these six consonants together, or what relation that was supposed to imply between truth and insistence. From my reading of Gandhi's writings and his life story, it seems that the term should be translated into Tibetan as '*Denpé Utsuk*' (i.e. 'insistence on truth'). In any case, correct or not, 'truth-insistence' has become general usage, and I too will follow that. 'Insistence' can mean 'emphasis', 'perpetuation', 'striving', 'obstinacy' or 'incorrigibility', of which the earlier definitions apply here.

b. 'Truth'. In Gandhi's thought, the nature of every individual's mind is virtue, which is to say, in Tibetan terms, the divinity that abides in love and compassion, joy and affection and peace, and this divinity is the one source of morality, right conduct, light and life, the soul of altruism beyond negativity and animosity, which is truth. From saying that this inexpressible and inconceivable divinity is truth, it follows that the expressible, conceivable truth is divine, that 'god' and 'truth' and 'soul' are different words for the same thing, and the divinity of truth is the greatly merciful one that gives life to all phenomena in the manifest world. The divinity of this eternal soul, or truth, embraces and abides in all, and is thus naturally present in the heart of each individual, where there is no other god than truth. The divine whose nature is virtue and the renunciation of sin, or truth, and non-violence are different aspects of the same thing, the nature of the soul or self, and the path of realising the essence of the soul or self, which he regarded as salvation. That is truth, the theoretical aspect.

c. 'Insistence'. The ascent of practice from below is inseparable from the descent of theory from above, and it is through this application of truth that individuals engage in the peaceful path. In the course of the political struggle for independence against British rulers inured to immorality, the use of non-violence called on them to regain their sense of truth, concentrating on bringing about a change of heart. Repaying good with good, like calming the rough with gentleness or repaying piss with tea, is as easy as doing normal business; but returning good for ill is the practice of hardship, and thus virtue, or (in Tibetan terms) like the deeds of Bodhisattvas, ready to do anything for the sake of truth, no matter how great the personal loss, fearless to the point of renouncing one's own life, undertaking hardship and enduring suffering with the discipline of a saint–this is insistence.

And insistence is practised for the sake of rights. When people's rights, the freedoms of body and mind, are violated forcefully by another, and they are made to suffer, the self-sacrifice of refusal to cooperate with the other, of disobeying, while abstaining from violence and conflict, this is insistence, meaning commitment and persistence, which is the practical aspect. Gandhi was a saint, who sought to unleash the inherently virtuous nature of the mind, his own and everyone else's; he worked dedicatedly to change the minds of individuals and groups in society driven by greed and wrongdoing, hostility and hatred, anger and aggression, focused on excellence in virtue. He lived in a state of grace that banished the lower states of body and mind. Moreover, he did not just speak the truth, but practised it too, making him one of the great sages in human history. These few words about Gandhi and others like him who made such great contributions to world peace and human rights may seem absurdly brief, but they are intended just to explain the terms, and I beg the reader's patience.

2. *The identity of man's essential divinity and the essentially virtuous nature of the human mind, core of the Satyagraha philosophy*

Gandhi's philosophy has elements of the philosophies of the Indian religious tradition, such as the Brahmanism and Hinduism that Buddhists refer to as 'religion of the outsiders', of Christianity and of Islam, as well as Buddhist elements, and elements from the Western tradition of political thought and humanitarianism, so it can be seen as a great confluence of ideas from East and West. In particular, the essential core of the philosophy of truth-insistence is the identity of man's divine nature and the virtuous nature of the human mind, and the main source of this idea is the Brahmanism that we call 'outsider', 'the other side' and 'heretical',[6] and specifically the Vaishnava tradition based on the teachings of Lord Vishnu.

Gandhi's mother 'was very religious, made daily offerings and worship at the Vishnu temple, said prayers before taking food and followed the Chaturmas, or four-month programme of devotional fasting', and his father also 'went to the temple and listened to the teachings, and used to recite the Bhagavad Gita every day'. So he came from a religious family, and this must have left an impression on him in childhood. As he wrote, 'I had faith in the teachings of Vishnu from the moment I was born.' Because the Vedic scriptures affirm the existence of a permanent, singular, autonomous soul, he wrote, 'I believe that the world and all its inhabitants were made by a creator, and that the permanent, autonomous souls of individuals are of the absolute divine nature ... that the self and the absolute are of one nature.' He also wrote that 'There is a power barely describable by philosophy and which I cannot see with the eyes of my gross body, but I can feel that it pervades all ... material objects are unstable and without even momentary permanence ... there is a power constantly present in this changeable matter, animating it, that embraces all the matter in the apparent world, that makes it grow and flourish, destroys it, and makes it grow again, and this spiritual power that animates and renews is none other than God.' 'That soul abides in all men, and exclusively seeks absolute truth', and 'I believe that the path of understanding the nature of the soul or the self is liberation, through which one can see the nature of God, and that is a fortunate condition, devoid of grasping and sin. It is my aim to cultivate the perfect moral conduct of the three doors (body, speech and mind) toward that end.'

With its philosophical basis in Vedic thought, Gandhi's philosophy accepted some fundamental ideas, like Karma, rebirth and Moksha from other Indian religious schools, including Buddhism, as well as from Christianity and Islam, for he declared that 'Religions are different paths leading to the same destination', seeing them all as perfectly benign approaches to truth, and realising them all to be compatible, so his thought was enriched by a variety of religious views and ideas.

Among his other sources of inspiration were the essay on 'Civil Disobedience' by the American writer H. D. Thoreau, as we have explored, and the Russian writer Tolstoy's 'The Kingdom of God is within You', where it is written that 'human beings are a form of life with discriminating intelligence, always striving for the knowledge of truth' and 'All men must inevitably traverse the path of truth, voluntarily or not', and 'the value of human life is to assist in the creation of heaven, which means serving the world. That service is the affirmation of truth by each according to his capacity, and the practice of respect for truth, through which it is eventually accomplished.' 'The kingdom of God has no visible form, it is not to be found either far or near, for the kingdom of God is within you.'

Another inspiration was the English writer John Ruskin, whose work of humanitarian philosophy 'Unto this Last' states: 'The good of the individual is contained in the good of all. The lawyer's work has the same value as the barber's, in as much as all have the same right of earning their livelihood from their work', of which Gandhi wrote, 'I was captivated. It caused me to change my life.' So his philosophy of truth-insistence was also influenced by Western ideas and humanitarian thought.

Thus the Mahatma wrote, 'It is through experiments with truth on myself and others that I have been able to travel a higher path' and 'I cannot remain without experimenting, and life is nothing other than a series of such experiments', and the view resulting from his experiments over a long period was of the identity of man's divine nature and the virtuous nature of mind. He saw an all-encompassing God, truth, light, soul and life as different manifestations of the same reality, which he considered to be the rejection of aggression, peace, loving kindness, compassion, joy and love, and although divided into divine and human aspects, were ultimately of the same essence.

> I have confidence in the absolute oneness of God, and therefore of humanity. One might object that we are composed of a series of aggregates, and those are indeed there, but the soul is one. The rays of the sun are many through refraction, but they have the same source... For I can see that in the midst of death, life persists, in the midst of untruth, truth persists, in the midst of darkness, light persists. Hence I gather that God is Life, Truth, Light. He is Love. He is the Supreme Good... Whoever truly has God's blessing in his heart will be without malice and hostile to none... From my experience in innumerable situations, I know that when the mind is filled with God and peace, hostility no longer arises. This has been attested by world leaders throughout history. This is not my achievement but the gift of God... My God abides not in the heavens, but is known from this world. He abides in your heart and in mine... Since God pervades all, he is also in the heart of each human being. That is why each human being is a manifestation of God.

To make Gandhi's words more comprehensible, compare them with the Buddhist saying: 'Sentient beings are Buddhas, but instantly defiled by obscurations. Once these defilements are cleansed, they are actual Buddhas', or 'What we call people are Buddhas. The Bhagavan (Lord Buddha) is not other than them.'

If we alter a couple of syllables to make it as follows: 'Every human being is God, but instantly defiled by sin. Once the sinful mind is purified, they are actually God' and 'What we call people are God. The divine realm is not other than them', this is both consistent with Gandhi's view and more easily comprehensible for Tibetans. Thus, if we do not see his philosophy of the identity of man's divine nature and the virtuous nature of the human mind as having profound meaning and as a complete theory, we can see its broad and vast relevance to human society and its humanitarian character.

For me, the characteristic features of Gandhi's philosophy are its broad and all-encompassing view, and its humanitarianism. It has humanity at its very centre, and is also concerned with God, the soul, life and truth, which he locates within morality, justice and love, or the essence of goodness, which itself embraces all. It seems to me that such a view is broad and inclusive, enriched by the values of human morality, and humane, in which God is not distant or humanity close at hand, and the precept that 'the human mind is divine, and humans the manifestation of the divine' affirms that apart from 'truth' there is no other mystery to human affairs, making open all the secrets of theology, making the hidden widely known, the non-apparent apparent, the unclear clear, and bringing them from the sky down to earth, to be comprehensible, compelling and applicable for ordinary people. Those such as Gandhi, who can conceive new ways of truth, transform his mind accordingly, and meanwhile demonstrate their practical application and make them accessible to a mass audience, are extremely few in our society, and Gandhi himself, more than rare, was unique.

3. *Non-violence and non-cooperation, the essence of Satyagraha in practice*

As this is an explanation of the practical conduct aspect, I feel it is necessary to start from Gandhi's own exemplary conduct.

Whoever holds a view justified by tradition, or any view with professed origins in antiquity, is generally well received, and if such a view is matched by disciplined and wholesome conduct, people are liable to respect it greatly, to the point of gaining faith in it, for that is the natural inclination of humankind up to now. This was clearly the case with Gandhi. As I have said, his philosophy was strongly influenced by traditional religious philosophies, and the conduct of one professing the truth of the identity of man's divine nature and the virtuous nature of the human mind is one of corresponding virtue, not merely preaching the truth but putting it into practice in all aspects. Just as the deluded mental states of living beings are enumerated as 84,000, so there can certainly be 84,000 types of proper conduct.[7] I shall summarise the innumerable varieties of good conduct into four basic types: stable conviction, self-discipline, perfect honesty and cautious prudence, and relate Gandhi's mastery of good conduct from a young age on that basis.

On the advice of a family friend and adviser, the young Gandhi undertook to continue his education in England. He was preparing to leave, when some of his family members got together and said that one who went abroad would never be able to keep up his religious observances; they therefore sought to ban their co-religionists from going overseas. They said his intention was completely mistaken, they discouraged him and pressurised him on grounds of religion and custom. Eventually, they said publicly: 'From today onwards, this misguided youth is expelled from our ranks', and drove him out of the clan. But he replied, 'No one can change my wish to go and study in England.' This firm commitment, at the age of just eighteen, to going to study in England demonstrates his firm convictions from even a young age.

Initially, his wish to study in England was also opposed by his mother, who told him: 'They say that people over there eat lots of meat and drink alcohol all the time, so how could your mother be happy with that? Everything will be ruined.' Seeing how worried his mother was, he promised not to touch meat, alcohol or women in England, and he kept his promise, which again shows that he had self-discipline from even a young age.

When he started secondary school, one day a school inspector came and asked the students to write five English words to test their proficiency in English. His teacher saw that Gandhi had mis-spelled the word 'kettle', and covertly signalled to him to copy from the students sitting next to him. But Gandhi thought that teachers should not encourage their students to cheat, so did not follow the signal. In the end, none of the students made mistakes except Gandhi, and they all mocked him; but he said: 'I could never learn the art of cheating', which shows his perfect honesty.

While studying in England, he wrote: 'Being meticulous about daily expenses, I used to record every penny I spent, even small things like bus tickets, postage stamps and newspapers, and I would add them up every night before going to sleep. I never lost the habit, and later on, when responsible for the expenditure of hundreds of thousands of rupees from public funds, I was scrupulously restrained, and from the expenditure on all the campaigns I led, no debts were incurred, and there was even money left over', which shows his caution and prudence.

Another trait is that he was ready to admit his mistakes and confess. As a boy, completely taken by the pleasure of smoking, he stole small change from a servant's purse to buy cigarettes, and other small amounts on many such occasions. When he was fifteen, he chipped a fragment of gold off his elder brother's ring for himself, but then felt so miserable about it that he vowed never to steal again, wrote a confession and presented it to his father. Far from getting angry or remonstrating, his father shed gentle tears, which seeped into the boy's mind, and it was from that time that he began to cultivate the great high-mindedness of non-violence, with its ability to transform the minds of others.

'I am very embarrassed by my own conduct, and have cried tears of shame over the slightest faults', he said, and had the utmost concern for correctness in conduct, for 'Moral conduct is the foundation of all, and truth is its essence. And the pursuit of truth is my sole objective', which is to say that the search for truth begins with one's own conduct. He was prepared to commit suicide rather than live without freedom, such was his love of freedom from a young age, beyond accounting here. If Gandhi himself observed such principled conduct as a child, what he did as an adult goes without saying. Throughout his seventy-nine years he demonstrated moral conduct visibly and tangibly in matters great and small from beginning to end, as can be seen from his life story; and those who wish to know more about this are encouraged to read it in detail.

In the above, I have described Gandhi's behaviour in his youth, and how it supports my recommendations. It is a shame that Gandhi was not born in Tibet. If he had been, he would have been, if not the 'second Buddha', at least an 'incarnation' with a title such as 'omniscient one' or 'lord of refuge' for his display of such perfect behaviour, exemplary in every way, from such a young age. Had Gandhi been a Tibetan, would such conduct not be considered as the sign of a superhuman 'incarnation'? The Tibetans would inevitably have recognised him as an incarnation of some kind.

In childhood, Gandhi was profoundly influenced by religious treatises, plays and stories, including the central Hindu scripture, the 'Bhagavad Gita'; the play called 'Shravana Pitribhakti Nataka', said to be another version of the Shyama Jataka story from the

'Bodhisattva-avadana-kalpalata',[8] which he saw as 'an example for me to follow'; and the story of 'Harishchandra', who made an unfailing promise to endure hardship for the sake of truth, similar to the story of King Drimé Kunden.[9] And yet he did not see himself as any kind of incarnation, nor style himself as anyone's spiritual master, nor did he claim that his asceticism was a religious practice. On the contrary, he stated that he would leave no religious creed or teaching as his legacy, and taught that everything should be decided with reference to its practical effect on this present world, human society, human rights, human nature, or in other words, universal human truths, just as individuals are judged by their actions.

This brings us to what has been termed 'non-violence and non-cooperation', and let us explore non-violence first. This term is in fact self-explanatory and widely known, but it seems to me that it implies a position of neutrality, non-commitment or even apathy and reluctance to act. At least, the words themselves give no sense of what it actually involves, other than the rejection of violence. I think the Chinese equivalent 'Fei Bao Li' (非暴力), meaning 'non-armed force' or 'non-violent conduct', does imply activity, and brings out the specific meaning of the term, but as keeping to the familiar meaning seems preferable, this definition is compatible with the most familiar meaning.

So the first thing that requires explanation is that as an action supporting the struggle for rights of whatever kind, non-violence is not like meditation, nor is it inaction and neutrality, still less reluctance to act or apathy. Rather, it is the enthusiastic undertaking of action requiring the willing endurance of hardship and suffering in order to secure rights. Of the dual aspects of exposition and accomplishment set out earlier, it is the latter, and it means working for the accomplishment of the goal without harming others, and expressing dislike, disapproval, discontent and lack of consent in a peaceful manner as a way of action. In short, it means undertaking any action with a pledge to endure hardship and remain patient in adversity.

Non-violence has at least two principles. One is that in the course of a struggle for individual freedom, equality and rights, one does not cause damage or inflict harm, as in the beating, smashing, looting and burning of life and property, whether government-owned, public or private. To do so is to infringe the rights and freedoms of others, of the other side, and it is wrong to damage the wellbeing of others in order to secure one's own. This is the principle of pacifism, and the other is that when in the course of a struggle for individual freedom, equality and rights, the other side (such as those in power), against whom the struggle is being conducted, cause damage or inflict harm, as in the beating, smashing, looting and burning of life and property, one does not retaliate. This means keeping to the Buddhist 'four precepts of training in virtue', not scolding back when scolded, not getting angry at the angry, not striking back when struck, not making counter-accusations when one's faults are probed. This is the self-imposed hardship of full asceticism and the perfection of patience, to the point of losing one's life sooner than losing one's temper. It is otherwise known as 'the courage to fill prisons', putting one's happiness in this life and one's life itself at risk for the sake of freedom, donning the armour of patience, and saying to the authorities, 'Open the doors of your prisons, we are coming in!', the keen pursuit of ascetic discipline. The objective is to awaken the moral conscience of the other side.

Gandhi is said to have instructed people in Satyagraha as follows: 'The Satyagrahi is without malice, can keep his temper, protests peacefully, does not fear punishment, is not afraid to go to prison, does not retaliate when arrested, does not answer back or hit back, and shows no aggression. During a protest campaign, Satyagrahis would not even consider shouting abuse or setting on those from the other side, even the leaders, and must even look after and spare those who abuse them.'

In the same way, Gandhi said that because 'Non-violence and truth are different names for the same thing ... by directly realising the truth that is in all and encompasses all, one should be able to generate the love of recognising even the smallest creature as one's equal.' 'That non-violence is true love is something I have read in our Hindu scriptures, in the Bible and in the Koran', and 'For me, love is only giving, with no thought of receiving anything in return. Love is only openness of spirit, without anger or thought of revenge.' Thus, 'The measure of true love is ascetic discipline, which means the deliberate acceptance of hardship', and he considered the cultivation of the boundless love of wishing all sentient beings to be happy and free of suffering to be the essence of non-violence. 'Just as violence is bestial, observing non-violence is one of the standards of human morality', and that is why 'I have made the vow, for my own benefit, never to use violence' and 'I am most happy to endure the suffering of imprisonment for the sake of my people.' In that way, 'Human nature is utmost similar, and I am certain that if one engages the other with trust and affection, they will respond with ten times more trust, and a thousand times more affection', so 'I can say without pride that this approach is essentially one of benefit to the entire world, and it is my practice.'

To take this as a cowardly approach is quite wrong, for as 'An attempt to undermine cruel intent through the power of the heart ... it is not for those with doubts or weak resolve, but for those with strength of mind ... it is specifically for the courageous, as I have emphasised time and again', because 'Weapons like knives and guns are for cowards', whereas 'fearless individuals whose courage is magnified by love do not use such things to protect themselves'.

Whatever happens, I must 'show love instead of hatred, self-renunciation instead of the will to harm, oppose armed force with a courageous heart'. 'Non-violence does not mean running away from confrontation with aggression. On the contrary, it means confronting aggression more energetically and sincerely than by responding in kind. By relying on the power of courage, or moral conduct, I am opposing immoral conduct. By all means, it wants to blunt the sword of aggression, rather than fight with someone holding a sharper sword. What they cannot believe is that I am not using weapons to resist. My offering the resistance of the spirit instead of armed resistance puts them in great difficulty. Initially they are astounded, but eventually, in desperation, they end up agreeing to our demands.' In this world, it seems that 'on one side is truth and non-violence, and on the other is falsehood and violence. These two cannot be reconciled', but in the end, 'Whether it is the freedom of an individual, of a people, or of the entire world, if that individual or people or world really employs non-violence, there is no doubt that they will reach their goal.' Such was his reasoning, which is quoted here in as much detail as we can manage here, but those who are interested in more are encouraged to read his works for themselves.

The second term is non-cooperation, or the refusal to regard, cooperate with or follow after power and authority. It is the same lack of confidence and willingness, refusal to follow and to respect, lack of voluntary acceptance, refusal of consent, of deference and service mentioned in the earlier discussion of 'disobedience', just expressed differently. It is translated into Chinese as 'Bu He Zuo' (不合作), 'non-cooperation' or 'non-collaboration'. This is easy enough for ordinary people to understand, but it is hard to come up with a term that is easy to pronounce in Tibetan, so I shall resort to the term '*Mitönpa*'.

Non-cooperation means non-cooperation with power and authority, principally turning one's back on the leaders and the government. Gandhi's view was that the British rulers concealed what was ultimately their greed and grasping by calling it 'progress'. For instance, reducing India to poverty with the introduction of various machines that benefited a certain few but ruined the livelihood of the majority, promoting conflict and filling the place with law courts and lawyers to tighten their hold on power and bring the masses under their control, hospitals and doctors that became an important means of making money and who killed tens and hundreds of thousands of animals every year in medical experiments, and so forth. This was equivalent to leaving their own country unspoilt while controlling subject populations for economic advantage.

British colonialism threatened to destroy the Indian traditions of noble and restrained conduct, the moral 'progress' established by the saintly forefathers of Indian culture. And whereas India had always been a united country with a single philosophy and way of life, the British practised 'divide and rule'. They called the Indians uncivilised, ignorant and backward, affecting to help them develop while actually intent on enslaving them, and blinding anyone who looked askance at their empire.

Now, said Gandhi, was the time for those educated in English, those who facilitated the subjection of India to British rule, to struggle for independence. Just as 'When one feels dissatisfied with an object one is using, one will simultaneously feel like getting rid of it', if we do not have rights, 'if you do not grant them, we will not remain as supplicants before you. Were we to do so, you would remain in charge. Rather, we will simply not associate with you.' 'If there is something I do not want to do, and I refuse to do it, that is resorting to Satyagraha', and 'If you act contrary to our will, we will not help you, and without our help, you cannot move one step forward.' Thus, when we do non-cooperation, not even your unjust laws will be respected, never mind other things. 'If I abide by any law I know to be wrong, that is a sign that I am not a man', 'For as long as we do not rid ourselves of the idea that we must follow unjust laws, we shall remain slaves' and 'The counsel that one should accept laws that one doesn't approve is anathema to thinking people, and to Dharma, and to accept wrong is a sign of being enslaved. If the authorities tell us that we have to dance naked in front of them, would we do so? As a Satyagrahi, I would say: 'You can keep this law for yourselves. I will not go naked in front of you, and neither will I dance.'

To list Gandhi's 19 points on the way of non-cooperation from his 'Hind Swaraj':

> We shall get nothing by asking; we shall have to take what we want, and we need the requisite strength for the effort, and that strength will be available to him only who will act thus:
>
> 1. He will only on rare occasions make use of the English language
> 2. If a lawyer, he will give up his profession, and take up a handloom
> 3. If a lawyer, he will devote his knowledge to enlightening both his people and the English
> 4. If a lawyer, he will not meddle with the quarrels between parties but will give up the courts, and from his experience induce the people to do likewise
> 5. If a lawyer, he will refuse to be a judge, as he will give up his profession
> 6. If a doctor, he will give up medicine, and understand that rather than mending bodies, he should mend souls
> 7. If a doctor, he will understand that no matter to which religion he belongs, it is better that bodies remain diseased rather than that they are cured through the instrumentality of the diabolical vivisection practised in European schools of medicine
> 8. Although a doctor, he will take up a handloom, and if any patients come to him, will tell them the cause of their disease, and will advise them to remove the cause, rather than pamper them with useless drugs; he will understand that if by not taking drugs, perchance the patient dies, the world will not come to grief and that he will have been really merciful to him
> 9. Although a wealthy man, yet regardless of his wealth he will speak out his mind and fear no one

10. If a wealthy man, he will devote his money to establishing hand-looms, and encourage others to use hand-made goods by wearing them himself
11. Like every other Indian, he will know that this is a time for repentance, expiation and mourning
12. Like every other Indian, he will know that to blame the English is useless, that they came because of us, and remain also for the same reason, and that they will either go or change their nature only when we reform ourselves
13. Like others, he will understand that at a time of mourning, there can be no indulgence, and that, whilst we are in a fallen state, to be in jail or exile is much the best
14. Like others, he will know that it is superstition to imagine it necessary that we must guard against being imprisoned in order that we may deal with the people
15. Like others, he will know that action is much better than speech; that it is our duty to say exactly what we think and face the consequences, and that it will be only then that we shall be able to impress anybody with our speech
16. Like others, he will understand that we shall become free only through suffering
17. Like others, he will understand that deportation for life to the Andamans is not sufficient expiation for the sin of encouraging European civilization
18. Like others, he will know that no nation has risen without suffering; that, even in physical warfare, the true test is suffering and not the killing of others, much more so in the warfare of passive resistance
19. Like others, he will know that it is an idle excuse to say that we shall do a thing when the others also do it: that we should do what we know to be right, and that others will do it when they see the way; that when I fancy a particular delicacy, I do not wait till others taste it; that to make a national effort and to suffer are in the nature of delicacies; and that to suffer under pressure is no suffering

From this, we can understand Gandhi's approach to non-cooperation. This supreme method pioneered by Gandhi, a branch of Satyagraha that later came to be known as 'non-cooperation' or 'passive resistance', has been joined by peoples in their tens and hundreds of thousands, one after another. Gandhi stated, 'Unless the British abolish the salt tax and the collectors return the money, unless Indians are given high office and British troops withdraw, we shall not use their machine-made goods, nor their English language. We shall not even use those factories', and he returned the offices and honours awarded him by the colonial government. He wrote a letter stating 'I have neither respect nor affection for a government that fosters impropriety in order to protect its own wrongdoing', whereupon all Indian supporters of independence renounced the titles and honours extended them by the British, walked out of British schools and law courts, stopped buying British products, staged large protest marches and meetings, and strikes by workers, traders and students. By not paying unjust taxes, obeying unjust laws and even abandoning their own livelihoods, non-cooperators caused the British colonial government severe losses. For instance, in the first non-cooperation campaign of 1922, Gandhi vowed not to buy British-manufactured cotton in order to promote the handloom industries of his own country, starting the hand-spinning and weaving campaign, after which imports of British textiles declined by 28 per cent, and production of Indian handloom products increased by 27 per cent.

Thus, non-violence and non-cooperation, the essence of the Satyagraha path that I have presented here, can be practised by all men and women regardless of their physical strength, and presents no bar even to children as young as fourteen, or invalids. It can be practised on a large scale by a whole nation, by hundreds of thousands joining together, or on a small scale by a single individual or household. Not wanting to quote too many of Gandhi's words, I have quoted just enough of them here. His actions were not a just a one-off; it took thirty years or more of repeated, sustained effort, but in the end the British were sent packing and India gained full independence.

4. *Gandhi's contribution*

I shall explain Gandhi's contribution from two perspectives: as a political activist practising religious values, and as an icon of the peaceful struggle for people's rights.

a. As a political activist practising religious values

I have not heard that Gandhi was profoundly accomplished in religious learning, but he does seem to have been an aspirant on the path. It seems to me that his skill in matching religious principles to political affairs and applying religious principles to politics, like pouring water into water, was his outstanding virtue, accomplishment and contribution. The innovation of Satyagraha, enriched by the philosophy of man's divine nature and beautified by the practice of non-violence and non-cooperation, being more than just the subject of discussion or contemplation, left an impression on the entire world, in terms of his own life, in terms of its impact on society, and especially in terms of its impact on politics, that was quite exceptional.

In the Tibetan way of seeing things, someone who is not a Buddha or Bodhisattva but who exemplifies the conduct of Buddhas and Bodhisattvas in the context of a struggle for rights, and who achieves things of benefit to all beings within the workings of society, is beyond the comprehension of ordinary people. Although in India at that time there were more religious schools than the hairs of a dappled horse, Gandhi was not a lama, nor an incarnation nor a spiritual teacher; but in the name of an easily comprehensible truth, the virtuous nature of the human mind, he joined religious causes to political ones, and political causes to religious ones, and carried 'insistence' on them through to the end. He was followed by tens and hundreds of thousands, and accomplished great political goals, and this is something scarcely believable for Tibetans. Nonetheless, it happened. For Gandhi's non-violent form of political struggle to spring from the soil of India, this ancient source of human civilisation, was not without its causes and conditions, and should be seen in terms of that particular context.

By one measure, while Gandhi's Satyagraha is of course seen as a means of political action, he himself saw it as a form of spiritual practice. 'Satyagraha' is a term taken from Sanskrit, in which 'Satya', meaning 'virtue, excellence, perfection' is simplified as 'truth', and the term 'Ahimsa' is also simplified as 'non-violence'. To put it in Tibetan terms, Gandhi turned the political struggle for human freedoms and rights into the practical application of the religious principle of doing no evil and practising virtue to perfection. Although he did not speak of what Tibetans know as 'seeing all sentient beings as one's mother', or things too large to comprehend, yet as human beings can hardly get along without depending on each other, and in their lives of mutual dependence keeping cordial relations with each other is the way of truth, and seeing the relevance of this to participation in political action, he considered that it was natural for humans to live in freedom, equality and love like family members, and that to harm each other was wrong, and demonstrated this in his own behaviour.

For example, during his Satyagraha campaigns, if ever he saw people engage in violence, he would resort to fasting, which he called 'the weapon of saints', to make them stop. He did this sixteen times in the course of his life, and during the struggle with the British he was 'delighted' to go to prison eighteen times for the cause of non-violence. On five of those occasions, he was in danger of assassination, but he said: 'If I have to die at the hands of a friend or brother, rather than of illness, far from getting angry, my wish to serve others would be fulfilled.'

During the Second World War, when the German Nazis had occupied Poland and the former Czechoslovakia and were slaughtering the Jews, he indicated to the latter his approval for resistance through non-violent non-cooperation; and when Churchill issued the call to the British people and the people of all territories under British rule to go to war against Germany, he said: 'Waging war is a violation of truth. If Hitler and Mussolini really want to, let them invade, but then you will need an efficient practice of Satyagraha!' At the time of Mussolini's invasion of Ethiopia, he pointed out that the reward for putting up with killing and destruction by others is greater than that of fighting, and on hearing that the government had surrendered to the invaders, he said: 'They have accepted the inevitable, and are to be praised for not becoming complicit in a senseless slaughter.' Thus he maintained the discipline of constantly engaging in virtue and abiding by the principles of Satyagraha.

He thought that those, even merciless rulers, who had not yet awoken their basic tendencies towards truth and love were bound to do so in time, and he once said: 'Whenever I lose hope, I tell myself that throughout history, truth and love have been the only victors. The evil rulers and murderers thrown up by history may seem invincible for a while, but their eventual defeat is in the nature of things—that I always remember.'

The way all the countries of this world handle conflict is brutal, nothing more than retaliation against one whom I claim to be my enemy. When the world loses its appetite for hostility and hatred and is looking for a way out of it, I would say decisively that the ancient nation of India, with its Satyagraha or bloodless revolution, has shown the world the way. My own view is that even if we have to wait for a long time, a freedom drenched in an ocean of blood is not what I want for my country; the fight must always be an exercise in non-violence, and I am busy preaching and practising the real 'union of religious and political (authority)',[10] or rather 'political and religious'.

Still, it seems to me that the seizure and control of power, oblivious to Gandhi's political thought, is generally the objective of politics, and the deceitful, underhand politicians who hold flexible pragmatism to be the highest principle of politics treated him with sarcasm and contempt, saying: 'To have a former lawyer turned advocate of the rabble, a naked fakir, joining in peace negotiations with the king-emperor's representative is nothing but a disgrace' (based on Churchill's words), and 'by all appearances, he seems to be unblemished by any of the common failings, but in reality he is fraudulent and devious' (from the script of the film *Gandhi*). He was falsely accused: 'There have been masses of do-gooders like Gandhi in the past, but in the end they succeeded in nothing but losing their appeal. They are against the people, they are imperialist stooges' (based on Stalin's words), and 'Politically, Gandhi was a great revolutionary, but as someone who wanted to revive religion and traditional culture, he was undoubtedly a reactionary in social terms'[11] (M. N. Roy, 1887–1954, Indian revolutionary, philosopher, political theorist and social activist); such are the criticisms made of him.

But over time, it was impossible for him not to command respect: 'Gandhi was not an imperialist stooge. He was someone skilled at teaching the masses, someone capable of correcting his own mistakes on the spot, someone who understood the requirements of historic progress, and therefore a people's president' said S. A. Dange (president of the Indian Communist Party) at the 1969 commemoration of the 100th anniversary of Gandhi's birth; and even his ideological adversary, the leader of the CPI(M) faction, expressed similar admiration for Gandhi on that occasion. As the French author and Nobel laureate Romain Rolland (1866–

1944) wrote, 'Saint Gandhi awoke his 300 million brothers and sisters and shook the British empire',[12] for Gandhi's theory of political conflict or non-violent path gave a great boost to the Indian independence movement and helped to turn the Indian National Congress from a modest forum into a popular mass political party, exerting heavy political pressure on the British rulers, and proved an excellent resource for the cause of Indian independence, capturing the sympathy of both East and West.

b. Icon of the peaceful struggle for people's rights

From the perspective of global political conflict, 'Satyagraha', as Gandhi called his approach, or non-violent non-cooperation, was effectively the source of the peaceful protest tradition. The innovation of an exceptional method for ordinary people to fight for their rights had a life-saving impact for all, and seems to have had a profound influence on the struggle for human rights ever since.

Gandhi noted how 'looking at the records of human history, one finds that from the very beginning, people have been at each others' throats, killing and wounding, fussing and fighting, not that they practised non-violence or lived in peace. If history consisted only of such things, humanity would have finished itself off long ago, and could not have continued as it has. It is a truth that people can live together in mutual non-aggression, amity and love. What I call truth power, mental courage or psychological independence is the truth for which I have searched history and not found, and it is non-violent by nature.' Meanwhile, those professing that 'Power grows out from the barrel of the gun', those who believe that victory is won through bloodshed, those who wield control through denying human rights, who jump at the chance to use violence clearly have no time for peaceful resistance, but Gandhi and other great figures have consistently relied on that practice, that path, that reasoning, that insistence to reach the goal of peace and instruct the world in truth.

Gandhi said: 'As I understand it, the reason why the rest of the world is so interested in our struggle is not because India is fighting for its own freedom, rather it is because of the unique methods of our freedom struggle, methods which no people in history are recorded to have used', non-violent methods that have their origins in ancient wisdom, that freed Tibet's neighbour India from British rule after less than two centuries without major bloodshed or loss of life, a great wonder of this world.

More generally, Gandhi conducted his campaigns of non-violence in exactly the same years as the fortune of the Chinese Communist Party was spreading across the world. The Communists proclaimed Marx and Engels' theory and view of the world, dedicated to removing private ownership of the means of production and building a classless and stateless society into which all existing class societies would eventually merge. They advocated the idea that the dispossessed of the world must be liberated from oppression and poverty. Using a revised version of this theory, subsequent politicians spoke of nation states adopting the socialist system, in which the proletariat or working class held power through dictatorship, and were the masters of the state, with Communist parties providing the actual leadership. The proletariat would smash the bourgeois political system through violent revolution, and build their own system in its place. Along with the liberation of the dispossessed, class enemies, the enemies of the socialist revolution and saboteurs of socialist construction must be eliminated, in order to establish a generally authoritative socialist system as an enabling condition for the realisation of communism. The whole world, from Europe to Asia, from Africa to the Americas, would be covered by a single Red order, 'rolling the four oceans and shaking the five continents', a single 'dictatorship' whose command is heard everywhere.

In India too, communist forces that approved of violence were on the rise, but Gandhi sat on the same level as the masses, and saw the propertied and the dispossessed, the high and the low, the best and the mediocre as equal, bearing the burden of solidarity with all. And since his 'Bodhisattva activity' of non-violent resistance had the support of all, the Congress Party to which he belonged and of which he was the leader was able to lead the entire country, not alienating any religious group, not stirring up any internal conflicts, despite India's large population (350 million at the time), and not threatening any of the small number of rulers (over 100,000 at the time) with death or injury, by resisting the controlling influence of violence. By contrast, 'violent proletarian revolution' in China threw up a mountain of corpses and an ocean of blood, open battles in which millions lost their lives. But who can deny that India was spared these horrors, due to the 'Great Bodhisattva', Mahatma Gandhi?

Still, there certainly are opposing views of Satyagraha and non-violent non-cooperation from various quarters, especially those in favour of flesh and blood and corpses, in favour of force, violence and absolute power, for whom Gandhi's political campaigns were incompatible with the nature, principles and character of proletarian revolution. For them, the idea of using non-violence in the course of a mass, popular revolution to temper extremism was a sign of weakness and timidity, crippling the enthusiastic determination of the masses, squandering the opportunity to make revolution and prolonging the struggle, like hammering down what sticks out or throwing water on the flames, and even worse, helping increase the prestige of the enemy. So there are those who oppose and challenge the principle of non-violence for taking the dynamism out of popular movements.

But at the time of Gandhi's death, fair-minded people were offering him high praise: 'He gave voice to the moral conscience of the world' (G. C. Marshall 1880–1959, US military and political leader, diplomat and architect of the post-war plan for European reconstruction, awarded the Nobel peace prize in

1953); 'As someone who believes in the love of humanity, Gandhi's death always oppresses me with sorrow and moves me to tears' (G. Bidault, French politician who served briefly as president); 'Generations to come may not believe that such a man as this ever walked this earth...To my mind, Gandhi's philosophy is superior to those of any other politician of our time. We should apply ourselves with his dedication, not depending on force to reach our goal, not collaborating with forces we consider abominable'[13] (Albert Einstein).

In particular, he was adored and respected by his successors: 'The light that has illumined this country these many years will illumine this country for many more years, and a thousand years later, that light will be seen in this country, and the world will see it, and it will give solace to innumerable hearts. For that light represented something more than the immediate past, it represented the living, the eternal truths, reminding us of the right path, drawing us from error, taking this ancient country to freedom'[14] (Jawaharlal Nehru, first prime minister of independent India); and on India's independence day, 15 August 1947, the legislative chamber of parliament paid a special tribute to 'Our guide of the past thirty years, philosopher and illuminator of India's path to freedom'.

So it is that Gandhi's Satyagraha, the non-violent non-cooperation form of political struggle, has established itself in political philosophy; moreover 'Gandhianism', understood as pacifism, seems to have become a universal doctrine of rights struggles throughout the world, and thus a complete philosophy in its own right. The Indian poet Tagore said that 'lasting human fulfilment is not found in the enjoyment of material things, but in dedicating oneself for the sake of an ideal more significant than one's own life, the ideals of motherland, people, God. These ideals make it easy for people to give up everything they have, their lives too. Before finding such ideals, humans must have been a mean-spirited lot, for it is these great ideals that free them from the ties of the material possessions in which they seek security.' This great ideal is unquestionably understood as Gandhi's example, which later become a universal philosophy. These days, the name 'Gandhi' is everywhere associated with peace and pacifism; he has become the icon of peaceful struggles to affirm rights.

Note: sources consulted on Gandhi include the Chinese translation of Gandhi's *Autobiography*, Naga Sanggyé Tendar's Tibetan translation of *Hind Swaraj*, Lhalung Losang Puntsok's Tibetan translation of *The Life and Collected Writings of Mahatma Gandhi*, and the film *Gandhi*, among others.

Non-violent non-cooperation in action

In terms of non-violent non-cooperation campaigns, Gandhi led four of them in all, and I will give brief accounts of each in order.

First campaign (September 1920-February 1922): the rise of the national liberation movement in India followed after the First World War, as one ocean wave generates another. Measures were taken to ensure the stability of British colonial rule, preparations for legal reform, and the distribution of sweeteners and enticements to Indian notables, including the aristocracy, on one side; and on another side came the launching of a crackdown following the announcement of the Rowlatt Act. (The Rowlatt Act prohibiting the national liberation movement was passed by the British colonial government in February 1919. It was named after its chief architect, the then serving British judge S. A. Rowlatt. The main points it contained were that in cases of arrest without a warrant, any Indian suspected of being an anti-government insurgent could be detained 'preventively' without trial, be searched, could be held indefinitely even without questioning, and was not permitted to contact a lawyer or guarantor to act on his behalf; that cases of suspected insurgency were to be tried without jury, by a panel of three government-appointed judges, with no avenue of appeal to a higher court; that the government could limit the size of a public gathering; that it could move 'bad elements' considered a threat to social order into designated accommodation; that it had the power to reinforce security provisions in any city, and that the police were authorised to disperse public gatherings and demonstrations.)

Following the Amritsar Massacre on 13 April 1919, far from being intimidated, the Indian people intensified their resistance to British rule. (After the announcement of the Rowlatt Act, anyone considered suspicious was arrested and detained, leading to popular protest against the denial of political freedoms. On 10 April, over 30,000 people gathered outside the municipal government offices in Amritsar city, and were beaten off by police and auxiliaries. On 13 April, a larger crowd of 50,000 gathered in peaceful protest at an open area in the city. The British officer in command, R. E. H. Dwyer, led 149 soldiers to the spot and had them fire a rain of bullets into the crowd. There are differing accounts of the numbers of dead and wounded: the figures announced by the government were 379 dead and 1,200 wounded, but the undertakers spoke of 500 corpses, whereas Dwyer claimed that the number of dead was between 200 and 300, and some estimates are as high as 2,000 dead and 3,000 wounded.)

In response to this incident, Gandhi planned a non-violent non-cooperation campaign for September 1920, with the avowed aim of pushing for Indian home rule. 'If possible, we will go for home rule within the empire. If necessary, for complete independence', he declared. Under his leadership there was a nationwide strike, schools and businesses remained closed, and there were widespread protest marches and public meetings, as if the flood waters had been released. On 5 February 1922, over 2,000 protesting farmers in the north Indian town of Charichara burned down a police station, killing 22 policemen inside. This was a violation of the non-violent struggle, and on hearing about it, Gandhi, on principle, called the campaign to a halt. On 12 February, the National Congress passed a resolution condemning 'unacceptable behaviour', and on 10 March Gandhi was imprisoned, and a severe crackdown imposed on the movement.

Second campaign (March 1930-April 1934): the effects of the 1929 economic crash in the capitalist world were also felt in India. The National Congress approved the launch of a popular non-cooperation movement proposed by Gandhi. The stated objective was independence for India, and the leadership of the campaign was entrusted to Gandhi. He decided to begin the campaign by protesting against a law prohibiting Indians from collecting and trading in salt. On 12 March 1930, Gandhi led a group of 78 committed participants on a protest march from Ahmedabad to the southern coastal town of Dandi, a distance of 388 km. They were joined by thousands of supporters along the way. The protest march went on for 25 days continuously. On 5 April, it reached the ocean shore at Dandi, where he picked up a handful of salt and held it up for all to see. It became known to history as the 'Salt March'. The rulers responded with an unrestrained crackdown.

On 5 May Gandhi was arrested. As a result, the nationwide protest campaign took on the form of a revolution, and there were anti-British uprisings in each locality, leading to 30,000 arrests. On 5 March 1931 was signed the Gandhi–Irwin Accord, also known as the 'Delhi Accord'. The colonial government agreed to scrap the law banning the collection and trade in salt, and the National Congress agreed to call off the agitation. That protest march became a classic example of victory for peace and justice over a powerful ruler.

Third campaign (October 1940-December 1941): after the outbreak of the Second World War, the British government of India unilaterally announced that India would also join the war effort. This displeased its Indian cadres, and the National Congress-run governments of seven provinces resigned one after another in protest. On 13 October 1940, Gandhi proposed a public non-cooperation campaign, and got his followers like Nehru and others to speak publicly as individuals against joining the war. In November, 30,000 Indian government employees were detained, another setback for the movement.

Fourth campaign (August 1942-May 1944): with the start of the war in the Pacific, the flames spread as far as India. Popular calls for independence increased. To contain the political emergency and consolidate their rule, in 1942 the British proposed an agenda for talks, but as it did not meet the National Congress' demands for the formation of a national government and for Indian control of national defence, the Congress decided to hold talks on Gandhi's 'Quit India' resolution instead. On the morning of 9 August, the British colonial government suddenly ordered the arrest of Gandhi and other Congress leaders. Over 60,000 were imprisoned, and the National Congress was banned. Gandhi was released on grounds of ill health on 6 May 1944. On 24 May, he announced the end of the campaign to drive out the British. Thus, these successive non-violent non-cooperation campaigns led by Gandhi ended with India gaining independence and following the democratic path.

Gandhi's campaigns led to a great victory in India, and had great influence around the world: for the Civil Rights movement led by Martin Luther King in twentieth-century America, for the Anti-apartheid movement in South Africa led by Bishop Desmond Tutu and others, as well as the Charter 77 movement led by Vaclav Havel and others in former Czechoslovakia, the Solidarity movement in Poland led by Lech Walesa, and the successive so-called 'featherdown revolutions' or 'colour revolutions', down to Aung San Suu Kyi, opponent of military rule and promoter of democracy in Burma, all of which can be followed up in other sources.

In summary

It seems to me that one should consider everything from the standpoint of universal values or, under the present circumstances, one could just as well say 'from the standpoint of politics'. That is to say, from the humanist perspective, taking humanity as its fundamental concern, human freedom, equality, justice, rights, democracy, value and life should be respected to the moral and evaluative standard of a civilised society, without discrimination as to nationality, race, religion or region, given equal recognition, and thought of in terms of universal values.

Thinking in that way, in relation to politics, since nothing is unrelated to politics, a method, a justification and a basis are also required, and that is Gandhi's Satyagraha, although everyone else might have realised this before I did. The right to civil disobedience, the philosophy of truth-insistence and the strategy of non-violent non-cooperation described in this chapter are different aspects of the same phenomenon, or different terms with the same meaning, but I have not so far seen this explained, so I have given my own account of the meaning of the terms. I like to think it is the product of my study and reflection, not something imaginary. In writing such a long and discursive essay, I had only one intention, and that is to give the most clearly comprehensible account of non-violence, or non-violent non-cooperation to give it its full name, in view of the real danger of falling into the abyss of extremism.

If those who consider themselves learned do not wish to lend their precious ears to the 'nonsense' spouted by a 'deviant' like me, that is fine, but I do request that you pay attention to Gandhi's ideas, for Satyagraha is without equal as a method for, and understanding of, the struggle for universal rights, which is why he became not just the 'guiding light' of India, but the 'moral conscience of the world'.

If Tibetans attained a high level of religious development as a result of 1,000 years of absorbing Indian religious culture, now their absorption of Indian (Gandhian) political culture could result in their winning political rights too. It's all a matter of universal values.

Without the Himalaya, we might think of India as a close relative, our religions being from a common source; but with the Himalaya, we speak of India as a distant 'heretic/outsider' and have developed a different political system. It's all because of religious ideas...

If, in ancient times, the Himalaya could have been simply flattened with willpower, truth-insistence is right nearby, a path of political action within arm's reach. It's all near at hand, within easy reach...

Say that the need to treat India as the source of secular wisdom, just as it is the source of religion, is determined by the 'Karma' of the Tibetan people if you wish, but it's all political...

The India of Gandhi's time, with the predominance of traditional religions, the way the colonial rulers considered Indians to be 'barbaric, superstitious, dark and backward',[15] and their uncontrolled brutality and oppression, is superficially identical with today's Tibet. The differences are that powerful political parties were developed in India, but not in Tibet; that the British rulers of India had some degree of moral conscience, which is not the case in Tibet; and that a Gandhi (a leader), equipped for the freedom struggle, appeared within India, while none has appeared in Tibet. Not that there are no reasons for this: the different international environment, changing times, and internal and external causes and conditions all have to be considered, but the main thing is that Gandhi's political activism was tolerated, no matter how much he talked politics, no matter how much he opposed the government. And even when he ended up in prison, far from taking his life, the authorities did not even deny him the right to have his speeches, writings and so on carried regularly by the media, because this was a political environment in which moral principles were respected.

Not to take these differences as an excuse, though, we should consider that we belong to the same religious and cultural sphere, and especially, thinking in terms of universal values, or in political terms, if intelligent methods are applied, they will yield the same results in all respects. This is because dissimilarity is rooted in similarity.

Whether or not there will be a Tibetan Gandhi, whether or not Satyagraha has any foundation there, whether or not non-violent non-cooperation will produce results, this we cannot know without an unfailing prophecy; but if the answer is to be affirmative, that prophecy is something that each Tibetan must keep in their heart. This is my belief.

What makes me uneasy is this: Gandhi's way is one of the major doctrines in social and political science. My fear is that this great marriage of method and wisdom, theoretically great, morally great and great in practical applicability, will be accepted in places like China only in its practical aspect, and the spiritual aspect ignored. That is to say, adopting the method of non-violent non-resistance while rejecting the theory of the identity of the virtuous nature of the mind and man's divine nature is, in short, like cutting Gandhi in two and getting only half of him (that half being of no use by itself). This is actually why I have tried to give a careful explanation of Gandhi's thought from the different angles of its origins, theory, practice, the campaigns, and his personal contribution. But what if the religious people, steeped in religious dogma, disparage it as 'at one with the wrong views of the Hindus, an indulgence in heresy'? What if the champions of self-interest who look to the Communist system for all their human rights decide that it is 'deviant' and 'reactionary', and send us to jail? And what if the lion-hearted braves curse it as 'an impotent weapon for weaklings'? This seriously disturbs me.

What embarrasses me, with my incomplete, shallow and unsure understanding of this political philosophy, easy to pick up but hard to practise, is having to 'continually repeat myself like a half-witted man, and grind the flour twice like a half-witted woman'.[16] In the case of Tibet, while it may not have much to learn in the wisdom aspect, if a new initiative for earnest and vigorous training in the method aspect were not to go as I would wish, or if, out of bloody mindedness, I provoke the opposite reaction, that would be even more embarrassing.

One thing to be pleased about is that signs of non-violent non-cooperation have been visible in recent years. I would say that it started in January 2006, with what I call the 'burning of decorative furs campaign';[17] but since the peaceful revolution in the Year of the Earth Rat, there have been incidents all over the three provinces of Tibet of peaceful protest, marches, petitions, farming strikes, candle processions, new year celebration boycotts, hunger strikes and so on, and one also hears chilling tales of protests made in desperation, like leaping into rivers and self-immolation.[18] These incidents occur at the individual level, at the group level, and society wide, yet cannot be established as a directed, planned, organised movement with a coherent ideology. Still, apart from a few displays of extreme behaviour, most were absolutely, undeniably acts of truth-insistence and non-violent non-cooperation. It is just a shame that Gandhi's 'Tulku' (reincarnation) has not shown up.

But one thing I can say with pride and dignity is that for a variety of causes and conditions, too many to mention in detail, there are signs that the Tibetan people are stumblingly starting to recollect their dormant inclinations towards political emancipation, such as freedom, democracy and individual rights. Therefore, if people can acquire the general sense of universal values, and learn the general methods of political protest compatible with them, there is little doubt that we will enter an era in which universal values are taken for granted. There are two reasons for this: one is that universal values are the highest good to which the world's people can aspire, and the other is that respect for universal human values is on the increase in all political systems, and will continue to be so in future.

CONCLUSION

Taking an overview, struggles for universal rights these days are not restricted to any particular region but have become a global phenomenon. The events in Tibet too became known worldwide: one might say 'the Tibet issue', or better 'the Tibet disturbances', or 'the Lhasa incident', but whichever, once the protests occurred, the dictators said, in denial of any Tibet issue, that Tibetans were enjoying an era of prosperity and Tibet was as stable as could be. We know that this is not so on the basis of the protests themselves, and the fact that they were so serious, which was quite clear. Before Tibet was again turned into a bloody arena of killing in this world, the importance given to the Tibet issue depended upon how forthright the world's politicians were prepared to be; but the fact that the history, situation and actuality of the Tibet issue are not only an issue to be discussed, but an issue to be decided on the basis of Tibetan popular will now goes without saying. At the very least, this issue has become one that cannot remain undecided.

Now that the Tibet issue has gone from being invisible to being visible, from unclear to clear, from non-existent to existent, and the international community is at least aware, whereas they paid no attention when no issue was being made, it has risen to a point where there is much to be said about it, and the advocates of universal rights have been greatly vindicated. The cause of the Tibetans is about respect for the principles of universal values, the core of human liberty, and the aspiration for a mutually beneficial and peaceful solution, with none of the animosity that will lead to ruin for both sides. But with the autocratic government 'standing on the wrong side of history' (US President Barack Obama's phrase), rejecting all discussion and impartial submissions without acknowledgement, there is not much hope. For that, I would say that finding a solution by looking inwards with self-confidence is the key.

From the internal perspective, Tibetans find themselves at a historic crossroads, where understanding which path to take is of utmost importance. With all the mistakes that have been made in the past due to not knowing which path to follow at the crossroads, they would do well to reconsider. In the past, Tibet had no historic architects of political strategy. Whether these will appear or not ultimately depends on whether popular consciousness and individual awareness is raised. For now, the gift from above of the seed of universal values in Tibet is a wonderful thing, and since the natural elements of water, fertiliser and sunlight are now needed for it to ripen and bear fruit, the strict avoidance of extremism is crucial.

Within Tibet, it is the case (at least in Amdo) that the truisms uttered by one simple-minded Lama have more currency than the counsels of a hundred wise laymen; so in terms of minimal tactics, at a time of confrontation, coming up with wise and intelligent responses is an urgent responsibility for all the 'living gods' there are in Tibet. I would say that at critical and dangerous moments, the deployment of good judgement and intellect is of still greater importance. In my own case, not having the courage to join the revolution has left me with a tormented conscience. For conscience to suppress fear requires a long and bumpy ride. Thus, with the citadel of freedom as the goal, and non-violent non-cooperation as the means, the mountain peak cannot be reached in a single bound; rather the route is made up of small steps, just as one does not attain enlightenment by instantaneously projecting oneself as a Buddha, but slowly slowly, over time, the way becomes apparent. We say such things, thinking it sober judgement, but these are mere words, just boasts in comparison with practical action, of no more use than the written word is to a musician, just a way to relieve the agonies of conscience.

But objectively speaking, if there are signs of the revolution continuing, the way of making revolutions today is 1) peaceful, 2) peaceful and 3) peaceful, as in the 'Rose', 'Orange' and 'Tulip' revolutions, whose participants carried flowers in their hands. I have heard that researchers who looked at over 300 different conflicts over the past 200 years calculated that of struggles waged with violence, 23 per cent were successful; but of those waged peacefully, 56 per cent achieved their aim, and this is serious research that deserves credibility.[1] So, if we are capable of non-violent protest with Khata,[2] rosaries or butter lamps in our hands, it seems to me that a revolution peaceful in both name and nature can be carried through in Tibet. However, what I would emphasise conclusively is that it is crucial not to stray onto the wrong path of violence, so my prayer is for both competence and constraint in the spreading of freedom.

APPENDICES

One: Universal values

According to philosophy and the human sciences, I understand universal values as the values and beliefs commonly recognised in moral and analytical terms by people in civilised societies as applicable to all, regardless of territory, religion, nationality or ethnicity. These are:

1. Social ethics—the view of the world as one household, and all humanity as brothers and sisters
2. Humanitarianism—the principle that humanity must be seen as the end, never as the means
3. Justice and equity—each individual has the right to equality of opportunity within his or her community
4. Equality and freedom—every human being is naturally equal and free. Equality and freedom are the innate rights of human beings, and are not granted by states, rulers, lords, Lamas or Tulkus. All human beings have the same worth as humans irrespective of race, skin colour, economic status, gender, religion, nationality or ethnicity
5. Human rights are granted by heaven, and the individual's prerogative is higher than that of the state. The purpose of having the state is to serve the individual; individuals do not live

to serve the state. The state has an obligation to protect the innate rights of individuals, such as the rights to livelihood, to live in freedom from fear, to have children, to information, not to live in absolute poverty, to freedom of thought, to express opinions, and to hold public meetings and marches. This is the purpose of establishing the state, and if a government does not deliver, the people can in time change it and overthrow it

6. Respect for all, so that I will not force what I myself dislike on others. The struggle for rights never crosses the line of not harming others
7. Democracy and rule of law—the 'people' are ultimately the true 'masters' of the state, and the government is nothing more than their servant. Office holders are invested with minor and temporary powers, but they are not the real owners of the state. It is imperative that those in power rule on the basis of established law, and it is not acceptable for individuals to enforce their whims and change the rules as they please, leaving the people, the masters of the state, at a loss
8. Respect for diversity—every people, every lineage, every culture has its distinct character. None is perfect, none is superior, and those that happen to be dominant at any given time should respect the languages and livelihoods of those different from themselves and treat them with tolerance
9. Respect for nature—there is only one planet. Human beings are no more than poor cousins and guests on this planet. Destroying the environment without restraint, for the sake of self-interest and convenience, and wiping out the earth on which other peoples, other forms of life and future generations have to live is not acceptable
10. Respect for living creatures—the lives of all living creatures are valuable, and not just the necessities of their lives but their right to live must be respected. Even when (interference with

their lives is) inevitable, the death of other creatures, and the fear caused them, should be kept to the minimum

11. There can be mutual tolerance with the 'champions of profit'. On the premise of not infringing the rights of others, we need to be open minded enough to let individuals be as ambitious and greedy as they like
12. There can be mutual tolerance with the 'champions of self-interest' too. Others also want what I want, and everyone needs the openness of mind to volunteer cooperation

These universal values are debatable, and it is through that debate that civilisation progresses; but the core principles, I believe, become clearer and firmer every day.

Two: the author's Tibetan translation of the Universal Declaration of Human Rights from the Chinese[1]

Three: Shokdung's published works

A Distant Appeal for Rationality (*dPyod shes rgyang 'bod*), Gansu People's Publishing House, 2001

His best known work, a critique of the blind acceptance of religious dogma and lack of critical thinking in Tibetan society. This is the theme of all three books.

The Courage to Doubt (*Dogs slong snying stobs*), Yunnan People's Publishing House, 2005

A humanist argument for individual conscience and intellectual scepticism.

Reasoning Solves All (*Rig shes kun grol*), Gansu People's Publishing House, 2008

Proposes that indigenous Tibetan religion involved a national/secular orientation that was suppressed and replaced by the universalist approach of Buddhism with its ideas of non-self and emptiness.

NOTES

FOREWORD

1. Lauran R. Hartley, '"Inventing modernity" in Amdo: Views on the Role of Traditional Tibetan Culture in a Developing Society', in T. Huber (ed.), *Amdo Tibetans in Transition. Society and Culture in the Post-Mao Era. Proceedings of the Ninth Seminar of the IATS, 2000, vol. 2/5*. Leiden: Brill, 2002, pp. 1–25.
2. Dan Smyer Yu', 'Subaltern placiality in Modern Tibet: Critical Discourses in the Works of Shogdong', *China Information* 27(2) (2013), pp. 155–172. While Yu's analysis is often valid, it omits to decrypt and unwrap Shokdung's fascination with Western values.
3. *The Courage of Raising Doubts* (*Dogs slong snying stobs*, Kunming: Yunnan Nationalities Publishing House, 2005); *Liberating Reasoning Consciousness* (*Rig shes kun grol*, Lanzhou: Gansu Nationalities Publishing House, 2008); *Inviting Critical Mind from Afar* (*Dpyod shes rgyang 'bod*, id., 2009).
4. A tulku (Tib. sprul sku) is a reincarnated lama.
5. On Khenpo Tsultrim Lodro's attempts at negotiating a Tibetan Buddhist modernism, see Holly Gayley, 'The Ethics of Cultural Survival: A Buddhist Vision of Progress in Mkhan po 'Jigs phun's *Heart Advice to Tibetans for the 21st Century*', in G. Tuttle (ed.), *Mapping the Modern in Tibet.* Sankt Augustin, Germany: International Institute for Tibetan and Buddhist Studies, 2011; Holly Gayley, 'Reimagining Buddhist Ethics on the Tibetan Plateau,' *Journal of Buddhist Ethics* 20, (2013) pp. 247–286.
6. For a survey of which see Robert Barnett, 'The Tibet Protests of

Spring 2008', *China Perspectives* 3, (2009), available at: http://chinaperspectives.revues.org/4836.

7. 'Invisible Tibet', http://woeser.middle-way.net/ (accessed 31 August 2016).
8. Kalsang Rinchen, 'Tibetan writer "Shogdung" released on "bail pending trial"', *Phayul*, 15 October 2010, available at: http://www.phayul.com/news/article.aspx?id=28351, (accessed 30 August 2015).
9. International Campaign for Tibet, 'Tibetan Writer Tagyal Released from Prison on Bail', 15 October 2015, available at: http://www.savetibet.org/tibetan-writer-tagyal-released-from-prison-on-bail/, (accessed 30 August 2015).
10. Wu Qi, a Tibetan intellectual otherwise very critical of Shokdung's positions on religion, concedes that Shokdung and his followers have 'had a positive influence on Tibet's publication language. The New Thinkers [Shokdung's school] have tried to build new terms into the Tibetan language', Wu Qi, *Tradition and Modernity: Cultural Continuum and Transition among Tibetans in Amdo*. Ph.D. Dissertation at the University of Helsinki, 2013, p. 268). On a discussion of Shokdung's crafting of new terminology regarding human rights, see Françoise Robin, 'Discussing Rights and Human Rights in Tibet', in Benjamin Hillman & Gray Tuttle (eds.), *Ethnic Conflict in Western China*. New York: Columbia University Press, to be published.
11. Don Lopez has amply described this phenomenon in *Prisoners of Shangri-la: Tibetan Buddhism and the West*, Chicago: University of Chicago Press (1999).
12. Glenn Mullin's introduction to *Death and Dying: The Tibetan Tradition* provides an example of an idealized simplification of Tibetan history and civilization, that strangely and comically echoes Shokdung's: 'While in the Western world etc'. (Glenn Mullin, *Death and Dying: The Tibetan Tradition*. London: Arcane, 1986): 'While we in the West were struggling through the Dark Ages and then barging through the world like madmen to colonise and seize other peoples' lands, the Tibetans were sat in their grottoes and monasteries, drinking their butter tea, eating their yak's cheese and quietly going about their studies, meditation and literary compositions.' It suffices to read Rachel M. McCleary and

Leonard van der Kuijp's summary of the rise of the Tibetan Buddhist sect Gelukpa to realize that the 1500–1600, which G. Mullin imagines as being populated by sages engulfed in pondering over life and death, was full of strife for worldly and spiritual superiority. Rachel M. McCleary and Leonard van der Kuijp, 'The Formation of the Tibetan State Religion: 1419–1642,' CID Working Paper 154, (2007), revised 2008.

13. For an edited English translation, see Nulo Naktsang (trans. Angus Cargill and Sonam Lhamo), *My Tibetan Childhood. When Ice Shattered Stone*. Langham: Duke University Press, 2014.

PREFACE

1. The 5th Dalai Lama, Ngawang Losang Gyatso, died in 1682 at the age of 65, but this was kept secret by his regent and disciple Désì Sanggyé Gyatso, largely to prevent manipulation of the recognition of his reincarnation by the Qosot Mongol allies of the new Tibetan state. The 6th Dalai Lama, Tsangyang Gyatso, was enthroned as a boy of eleven in 1694.

TERMINOLOGY

1. Originally quoted in Thucydides, *History of the Peloponnesian War*, Book 2, Chapter 44.
2. Earth Rat 2008 was the 50th anniversary of a major uprising against the introduction of Communist 'reforms' in the province of Amdo, north-eastern Tibet, which was crushed by the PLA. Countless thousands were massacred in military assaults on civilian populations; most of the adult male population was incarcerated in concentration camps that few survived; monasteries and communities were destroyed.

1. JOY

1. From the Era of Fragmentation, between the ninth and eleventh centuries, when the political centralisation of the earlier Tibetan Empire collapsed.
2. The Four Noble Truths of suffering, the cause of suffering, the cessa-

tion of suffering and the path are believed to be the first teaching given by Buddha Sakyamuni. In traditional commentaries, they are sometimes explained in four different aspects. 'Parting from the Four Attachments' is a teaching in the 'mind training' genre by the twelfth-century Sakya Lama Sa-chen Kunga Nyingpo. The four attachments are to the present life, to cyclic existence, to one's own benefit, and to grasping at phenomena as real.

3. The Magna Carta Libertatum or Great Charter of Liberties of England limited the absolute power of the monarchy, and came to be seen as an early foundation for constitutional law. Tibet was formally incorporated in the Mongol Yuan empire in 1260. The establishment of great monastic principalities in central Tibet took place through the thirteenth century.
4. The first Jamyang Shépa Ngawang Tsöndru (1648–1721), founder of the Labrang Tashikhyil monastery. His most celebrated treatise, the 'Great Exposition of Philosophical Tenets', is concerned with differentiating the variety of classical non-Buddhist and Buddhist philosophical positions on the nature of reality.
5. The Ambans were Manchu imperial representatives, first stationed in Lhasa in 1728, following a period of political upheaval.
6. The Panchen Lama was invited to Beijing as the most senior religious figure associated with the Lhasa government, the 8th Dalai Lama having barely attained his majority. The invitation actually seems to have been issued in 1778, in anticipation of the emperor's 70th birthday, and the Panchen, an experienced diplomat, accepted it apparently as an opportunity to promote Tibet's interests by giving teachings to the nominally Buddhist Qing court. This was in accord with the notion of 'priest–patron' relations favoured by the Tibetan establishment of the day, as the author notes rather scathingly. It turned out to be Palden Yéshé's last such opportunity, however, for he died of smallpox in the imperial capital in 1780, at the age of 43. In any case, despite the diplomatic efforts of Tibet's high Lamas, the Qing state was determined to increase its control over Tibetan affairs, and used the incident of the Gorkha invasion twelve years later to send in troops and enlarge the role of its Lhasa representatives [Amban], hence the edict mentioned here.

7. The 4th Lama Tsenpo incarnation (1789–1838) compiled his account of the world in Beijing in 1820, apparently after consulting numerous foreign language works in libraries there. His birthdate is hardly the most notable event in Tibetan history coinciding with the French revolution, but the author's point is that a secular literature and outlook was still unknown to Tibetans in the early nineteenth century.
8. The four-member 1948 Trade Mission was a belated and forlorn attempt by the Lhasa government to raise its international profile, as well as to negotiate trade protocols with newly independent India. It also visited Britain, the USA and China.
9. Dungkar Losang Trinlé (1927–97), educated as a Lama in the old society, and then trained as an academic under Communism, emerged during the 1980s as one of Tibet's leading historians. This encyclopaedia of mostly religious and historical terms, compiled from his collected notes, was published posthumously.
10. 10 March 1959, when Tibetans in Lhasa staged a decisive protest against Chinese rule, leading to the flight of the Dalai Lama and his court, has been commemorated annually by Tibetans in exile, and remains a sensitive date for the ruling Communist Party. On that day in 2008, Drepung monks staged a protest march from the monastery towards the city, sparking further monastic protests over the following days, culminating in a city-wide riot on 14 March, itself the spark for freedom protests all over Tibet during the following weeks. See also notes 28 and 38.
11. Tö Ngari is the high plateau of upper west Tibet, bordering the western Himalaya. Mé Doekham refers to the vast region of eastern Tibet, Amdo in the north-east, bordering the former Chinese provinces of Gansu and Sichuan, and Kham in the south-east, bordering Sichuan and Yunnan.
12. These are colloquial phrases in the author's native Amdo dialect, expressing the value placed on ancestral territory. The sheep's breast is considered the prime meat on the carcass.
13. Avalokitesvara is the Bodhisattva of compassion and the patron saint of Tibetan Buddhists. Mount Sumeru is the axis of this world system according to classical Indian cosmology, and on its peak is thought to

be a divine realm. Amitabha is the red Buddha of the west, a popular devotional figure in Chinese Buddhism.

14. Unidentified quotation. Kailasa is the famous mountain in upper west Tibet sacred to all Indian religions, and known in Tibetan as Kang Tisé.
15. 'Imperial times' is a reference to the Purgyal empire of the seventh to ninth centuries which unified the peoples of the Tibetan plateau into a state and a military power, the strongest in central Asia at that time. In his previous books, the author has argued that this indigenous Tibetan sense of nationhood and martial pride became eroded by the universalist and selfless values of Buddhism, leaving Tibetans ill-equipped for the transition to modernity.
16. '61 divisions' [*sTong sde* in Tibetan, or 'communities of a thousand'] is a stock phrase in some histories of the Tibetan empire, referring to the organisation of military units in each region. The source of the 'upper, middle and lower divisions' in the following paragraph is less clear.
17. Mount Meru, the axis of the universe in ancient Indian cosmology, is often used as a metaphor for the weight of the whole world in traditional literature.
18. 'Yellow-haired monkeys' is a pejorative reference to the peoples of modern western Europe and their history of building a new global economic order through colonialism and industrialisation.
19. It is hard not to read this judgement as a dismissal of the 'Middle Way' approach advocated by the Dalai Lama and the Tibetan government in exile, although it is aimed at the supposed ineffectiveness of civil society initiatives for democracy and rule of law in mainland China. For a summary of the approach, see the Tibetan government in exile website, http://mwa.tibet.net/
20. Liu Xiaobo was sentenced in 2009 to eleven years for his involvement in Charter 08. A year later, less than a year after this book was published, Liu Xiaobo was awarded the Nobel peace prize.
21. It is recorded in classical histories that following the collapse of the Purgyal empire in the mid-ninth century, popular revolts (Tibetan: *Kheng log*) took place against the restoration of imperial authority, at least in central Tibet.

22. Om Mani Padme Hum is the Mantra of Avalokitesvara, which is given high importance in Tibetan Buddhism and is much recited, especially by ordinary believers.
23. *The Liberty of Ancients and Moderns*, Commercial Publishing House, 1992, p. 294.
24. The five exiled Tibetan non-governmental organisations are the Tibetan Youth Congress, the Tibetan Women's Association, the Guchusum ex-political prisoners association, the National Democratic Party of Tibet, and Students for a Free Tibet (India).
25. TAR Party secretary Zhang Qingli used these words in an interview with state media a few days after the 14 March riot in Lhasa, while explaining the official view that it had been instigated by separatists in exile.
26. Pro-Tibet protests marred several stages of the 2008 global Olympic torch relay, especially in London, Paris and San Francisco in April. Counter-demonstrations were also organised by mobilising Chinese students, especially in the USA and Australia.
27. The source of the well-known 80,000 'mass incidents' figure seems to be a Chinese Academy of Social Sciences estimate for 2007. These figures are openly reported by state media, usually citing academic or public security data, and the numbers have continued to rise steeply since then.
28. 4 May 1919 was the day when nationalist Chinese students protested, in front of the Tiananmen gate, against the failure of the new republic's negotiators to secure China's basic demands at the Versailles international peace conference. The 'May 4th movement' is another name for the 'New Culture movement' of those times, advocating modernisation and acceptance of Western values.
29. 'Reform and Opening Up' is the official phrase coined for the liberalisation of the Maoist order in 1978–9, involving decollectivisation, the release of those imprisoned as 'counter-revolutionaries', promulgation of a new constitution, the 'Socialist Market' economy, and partial lifting of restrictions on contact with the outside world.
30. 4 June 1989 was the day when the CCP moved to end a two-month-long nationwide pro-democracy movement by ordering the army to clear

Tiananmen Square, which had been occupied by thousands of students calling for political reform. Despite the author's dismissive tone, it was the major turning point in relations between the CCP and China's citizens since the 1978 announcement of 'Reform and Opening Up'.

31. The brief uprising against Chinese rule in Lhasa in March 1959 was suppressed by the PLA shortly after the flight of the Dalai Lama and his court into exile. Thus ended nearly eight years of political cohabitation between the CCP and the former Tibetan government, leading to swift imposition of 'Democratic Reform', or the violent expropriation of propertied classes and the dismantling of monasteries and all other traditional institutions. Nationalist protest re-emerged in Lhasa in September 1987, some five years after the reforms reached Tibet. On 5 March 1989, with tensions in Lhasa high following the premature death of the 10th Panchen Lama in January and official banning of the Monlam Chenmo prayer festival in February (due to serious rioting the previous year), a riot broke out and continued for three days until the authorities declared martial law and closed the province to outsiders for over a year.
32. Tibetan areas of the PRC are divided between five provinces: the Tibet Autonomous region, Qinghai, Sichuan (Ganzi and Aba prefectures and Muli county), Gansu (Gannan prefecture and Pari county) and Yunnan (Dechen prefecture). The total area accorded 'Tibetan Autonomous' status is approximately 25 per cent of the entire PRC territory.
33. A 'Tulku' is a recognised reincarnation of a recently deceased lama. This sentence implies a cynical view that religious institutions benefit financially from installing reincarnate Lamas, who attract the faithful and their donations.
34. This phrase conveys timidity or half-heartedness, using a mild panacea instead of a specific and potent cure.
35. This is a phrase conveying inability or unwillingness to think for oneself.

2. SORROW, SHACKLED BY THE MANIFOLD CHAINS OF REPRESSION

1. Hu Xi (1891–1962) was an influential writer and philosopher, a leading figure in the May Fourth and New Culture movements, noted for

his contributions to Chinese language reform, who served as president of Beijing University, Nationalist China's ambassador to the USA, and later president of the Academia Sinica in Taipei.

2. Bapa Puntsok Wanggyé, who died on 30 March 2014, was one of the more idealistic early Communist officials who played a key role in Sino-Tibetan diplomacy in the 1950s, before falling victim to the Anti-Rightist campaign and then spending eighteen years in Qincheng maximum security prison. His life story, ghostwritten by Melvyn Goldstein, was published in English in 2004: Melvyn C. Goldstein, Dawei Sherap and William R. Siebenschuh, *A Tibetan Revolutionary: The Political Life and Times of Bapa Phüntso Wangye*. California: University of California Press, 2004.
3. The 70,000 Character Petition presented to the senior leadership in 1962 by the young 10th Panchen Lama is one of the most significant documents in modern Tibetan history, a careful but honest protest against the implementation of Democratic Reform, which led to his downfall, public denunciation and eventually the same Qincheng prison, for some nine years. It was translated into English and published by the now closed Tibet Information Network in London in 1997.
4. China signed the International Covenant of Civil and Political Rights (ICCPR) on 5 October 1998, but has yet to ratify it, despite repeated promises to do so.
5. The figure of 1.2 million unnatural Tibetan deaths during 1958–78 was produced by the information department of the exile government. It is a rough estimate largely based on oral interviews and guesswork, although it has since been treated as established fact by spokespersons for the Tibetan cause, and the challenge of producing a more accurate figure has yet to be met. The fact that it is unscientific does not necessarily mean, however, that it is too high; as the author notes, it could even be conservative.
6. The passage actually reads rather differently: 'In particular, as a result of them deliberately moving those prisoners to places with an environment to which they were not accustomed, huge numbers of people died from abnormal causes, creating a phenomenon where not all the prisoners' corpses could be buried. Therefore, hundreds of thousands of

parents, wives, children, friends and relatives of those who died of abnormal causes were extremely grieved' ('A Poisoned Arrow: the secret report of the 10th Panchen Lama', London: Tibet Information Network, 1997, p. 102). The wording may be convoluted because the Panchen was alluding to mass deaths from starvation in the prisons, something that could not be stated directly to the Party leadership at that time.

7. Jamdo Rinchen Zangpo, *Nga'i pha yul dang zhi ba'i bcings grol* (My Homeland and the Peaceful Liberation), *Nga'i pha yul dang gzab nyan* (Listening to my Homeland). Both books were published privately in Qinghai in 2008, and subsequently banned. See Chapter 2, note 7.
8. Jamdo Rinchen Sangpo is a monk author from the grasslands south of the Machu river, now part of Trika county in Tsolho prefecture, Qinghai. His two books recording community elders' memories of the 1958 revolt and its suppression, *My Homeland and Peaceful Liberation* and *Listening to my Homeland*, were published in 2008. He was arrested the following year and released months later on medical grounds, apparently due to ill treatment in custody.
9. 10 March 1959 was the day when thousands of Tibetans in Lhasa gathered outside the Dalai Lama's summer palace, following a rumour that he was to visit the PLA camp without bodyguards. Commonly described as an anti-Chinese uprising, it was actually a popular protest against the Tibetan cabinet ministers and other senior members of the traditional government, who were seen as collaborating with the CCP and betraying the country's basic interests. After the establishment of an exile community in India, 10 March became the main anniversary in the official calendar.
10. Dharmapala is the Sanskrit term for powerful spirits bound by great Buddhist masters to protect the teachings and their followers from harm, and they are traditionally propitiated especially in times of danger. Daka and Dakini are the nymphs and angels of Tantric Buddhism, usually seen as assisting the practitioner in gaining mystic realisation, rather than protecting believers from danger.
11. Melvyn Goldstein, *A Tibetan Revolutionary: the political life and times of Bapa Phuntso Wangye*. Berkeley: University of California Press, 2004.

12. Labrang Jigmé's testimony appears in a video broadcast by VOA on 3 September 2008. The English translation of this passage reads: 'A young soldier pointed an automatic rifle at me and said in Chinese, 'This is made to kill you Ahlos (derogatory term used for Tibetans by some Chinese). You make one move, and I will definitely shoot and kill you with this gun. I will throw your corpse in the trash and nobody will ever know.' VOA's full English translation of the video testimony is available at http://highpeakspureearth.com/2008/voa-video-testimony-of-labrang-monk-jigme/
13. Jamyang Kyi, *A Sequence of Tortures: A Diary of Interrogations*, available on Kindle, published by the Tibetan Women's Association in Dharamsala, India, June 2013.
14. Jamyang Kyi is a singer, author and well-known personality on Qinghai TV. She was detained for several weeks in the aftermath of the 2008 protests on suspicion of sharing information about the events. After her release, she published a diary of her detention experiences, from which these quotations are drawn.
15. Te'urang is the pen name of Tashi Rabten, a young writer from the Dzorge region of Amdo, who was a student at the Northwest Nationalities' University in Lanzhou at the time of the protests. He edited a special issue of the literary magazine *Shar Dungri* dedicated to the subject, and subsequently published a short and widely read book, *Written in Blood*, calling for civil liberties and equality for ethnic minorities. He was arrested in July 2009, sentenced to four years in 2011, and released in March 2014.
16. Gartsé Jigmé is a monk author from the Rebkong region of Amdo. His reflections on oppression and the struggle for justice were published as a book, *The Courage of the Emperors*, in 2008. He was arrested in 2013, shortly before the second volume of this work was to be published, and sentenced to five years in prison. Gartsé Jigmé's third book, which was seized by police from the publisher before printing, includes a discussion on the self-immolations in Tibet and Chinese policy, sources say. Gartsé Jigmé Gyatso was detained by police in his room at Gartse monastery in Tsekhog (Chinese: Zeke Xian) county in Malho (Chinese: Huangnan), Tibetan Autonomous Prefecture, Qinghai on

3 January 2013 and taken to Xining. Gartsé Jigmé, who began his writing career in 1999 after study for a monastic degree, was sentenced to five years in prison on 14 May 2013. Gartsé Jigmé had been under constant surveillance and detained a number of occasions since the publication of his second book in 2008, a collection of essays in the Tibetan language about the political situation in Tibet since the March 1959 Uprising and the protests that swept across Tibet in 2008. In one essay, translated into English by the International Campaign for Tibet, he wrote: 'When I think about these things, it seems to me that the political protests in many places in central Tibet, Kham and Amdo this year [2008] were not organized by the Dalai Lama but were the inevitable expression of the pain stored up for so long in the minds of Tibetans young and old.'

17. Tsering Dondrup was head of the literary bureau in Henan Sokpo county, Rebkong, when he published his novel on the fate of his homeland under Maoist rule in serial form in the Qinghai provincial Tibetan language newspaper in 2006. He was dismissed from his post in 2009, and the publication declared illegal. Tsering Dondrup, *Rlung dmar 'ur 'ur* (Raging Red Wind), 2006.
18. During the 'revolutionary' period of Communist rule (1949–78), individuals considered 'counter-revolutionaries' and 'class enemies' were given labels or 'hats', which qualified them for social exclusion and persecution.
19. The 10th Panchen Lama Choki Gyaltsen (1938–89) was a nominal supporter of the CCP and its 'peaceful liberation' of Tibet in his youth, and his 70,000 Character Petition suggests that he still held out hope of the leadership honouring its promises to minority nationalities and curbing left extremism, even after the experience of 'democratic reform' 1959–61. His hopes were dashed, however, once Mao Zedong returned to power at the centre in late 1962, and used his Petition as the reason to purge him. After being 'struggled' by the TAR Party in September–December 1964, he was moved to Beijing, 'struggled' again during the Cultural Revolution, and finally incarcerated in 1968 for the next nine years. He was formally rehabilitated in 1978, and returned to his former prominence as a political and religious leader until his premature death in January 1989.

20. See, for example, Human Rights Watch, 'China: Hundreds of Tibetan Detainees and Prisoners Unaccounted for', 9 March 2009, https://www.hrw.org/news/2009/03/09/china-hundreds-tibetan-detainees-and-prisoners-unaccounted (accessed 31 August 2016).
21. The 11th Panchen Lama, Gendun Choki Nyima (born in April 1989), was recognised by the Dalai Lama as the reincarnation of the 10th Panchen Lama in May 1995 in the course of a search process conducted with the tacit collaboration of the central government. This announcement was immediately rejected by the Chinese government, and three days later the Dalai Lama's candidate and his family members were taken from their home by Chinese officials and have not been seen since. In November 1995 the Chinese government's candidate, Gyaltsen Norbu, was enthroned as 11th Panchen Lama. Repeated requests by bilateral and international interlocutors for information on Gendun Choki Nyima's whereabouts over the following years have been dismissed by the Chinese authorities.
22. According to Tibetan medicine, cerebral afflictions such as stroke and epilepsy are caused by the malefic influence of the planet Rahu.
23. Chapels for the propitiation of the Dharmapalas or wrathful protector deities are to be found in all Tibetan monasteries, wherein it is common to keep disused weapons, usually swords, spears, muskets and so forth, as offerings to these deities. It is a tradition for hunters and soldiers to give up their weapons for this purpose as an act of religious renunciation.
24. Steamed meat dumplings.
25. This perception has only intensified since Shokdung wrote this book with the imposition of 'counter-terror' measures across Tibet, despite the absence of violent insurgency. The counter-terrorism drive in Tibet has a particular political dimension, involving training of police in Buddhist monasteries, the characterisation of religious teachings by the Dalai Lama as incitement to 'hatred' and 'extremist action', and the implication that Tibetan self-immolations can be characterised as 'terrorism'.
26. A location in the grasslands of Trika, western Amdo, now in Hainan prefecture, Qinghai.

27. Quotations from Jamdo Rinsang's *Listening to my Homeland.*
28. Ibid.
29. Dum-dum bullets cause a high degree of death and injury. Although no larger than an adult human finger, on hitting the target they explode, so that even a slight bullet wound causes major injury, and no one shot by one survives. They are named after the British military factory in India where they were produced. They were banned internationally in 1899.
30. Also from Jamdo Rinsang's *My Homeland and the Peaceful Liberation.*
31. Ibid.
32. Yung Lhundrup, a budding teenage writer from the Kangtsa pastoral region in north-west Qinghai, was a student at the Chentsa county middle school in October 2008 when he committed suicide by jumping from the roof, apparently in despair at the plight of the Tibetan people following the crackdown. A collection of his work entitled *Tibetans Languishing in Jail* was published posthumously.
33. *Fortunes of a Naktsang Kid* is a groundbreaking autobiographical work published privately in Qinghai in 2007. Naktsang Nulo, a retired local government official, recalls his childhood experiences of the 1958 revolt and aftermath in a naïve and personal style, belying the dangerously political content of his subject. The book was only belatedly banned in China.

3. FEAR OF EXTREMISM ON ALL SIDES

1. This was stated, for example, by Serbian Foreign Minister Vuk Jeremic at a UN Security Council meeting on 11 March 2008. UN Security Council, '"Kosovo Shall Remain A Part of Serbia Forever", says Serbia's Foreign Minister, Telling Security Council Independence Declaration "Illegal and Illegitimate"', 5850th Meeting (PM), 11 March 2008, SC/9273, http://www.un.org/press/en/2008/sc9273.doc.htm (accessed 31 August 2016).
2. This famous phrase is taken from the text of the 821 peace treaty between Tang China and Purgyal Tibet inscribed on stone pillars in Chang'an (present-day Xian), at the Gongbu Meru border (in the north-east of present-day Qinghai province), and in front of the main temple in Lhasa (still extant).

3. Te'urang's book (pp. 88–91) lists four instances from state and foreign media coverage of 14 March in Lhasa, showing that the violence was deliberately instigated by the authorities. These are claims by eyewitnesses or based on examination of film footage that the rioters who led attacks on property on 14 March were actually members of the security forces dressed as Tibetan monks and laymen.
4. Unsourced quotation.
5. A reference to the Tibetan saying: 'Tibetans are ruined by hope; Chinese are ruined by suspicion.'
6. These clichés are attributed to Mao Zedong and Joseph Goebbels respectively.
7. Tsering Woeser (born 1966) is a Beijing-based writer and poet of mixed Chinese and Tibetan descent, and perhaps the only outspoken Tibetan critic of the régime to have avoided incarceration thus far. Her Chinese language website, which is banned in China, has become a widely respected and valued source of critical reportage on contemporary Tibet. The quotations in this passage are from Chinese 'netizens' approving the state's use of violence in response to the 2008 protests.
8. The Hui people of Ningxia are China's largest and best integrated Muslim minority. They are commonly stereotyped as canny or even ruthless traders, and reputed for establishing successful migrant business communities in towns and cities all over China. They have enjoyed a significant but much resented presence in Tibetan areas since the 1980s economic liberalisation.
9. 'Dalai' is a deliberately disrespectful form of address for the present 14th Dalai Lama, commonly used by Communist leaders and in the official media.
10. The Tibetan general Ngenlam Takra Lukong led his army to the gates of the Tang capital in 763, at one of the high points of Tibet's career as a military power. Takra Lukong was depicted by the subsequent historiographical tradition of Buddhist Tibet as a supporter of the indigenous Bon religion and opponent of Buddhism and hence, one might suppose, a cultural hero for secular nationalists, although this characterisation is not historically reliable.
11. Gar Tri Tring Tsendrö, the middle son of Lönchen Gar, succeeded

his brother as Lönchen (chief minister) during emperor Dusong Mangpojé's minority, and famously led Tibetan troops to victory over Tang China in 696–8. Shortly after, by some accounts, fearing that the Gar family's power was superseding that of the royal family, the emperor isolated Gar by inviting his élite troops on a hunting expedition and massacring them, having negotiated a peace with China behind his back. When Dusong's army then came after Gar, he committed suicide rather than take up arms against his master, and the Gar family line ended with him. The story was passed down in Tibetan history as a proverbial instance of loyal service to the state being rewarded with treachery.

12. The author faced such criticism of his views in 1999 after the publication of an article entitled 'A blood-letting to eliminate the tumour of ignorance' in the Qinghai provincial Tibetan-language newspaper, arguing that the hold of traditional ideas and religious dogma was the main cause of the backwardness of the Tibetan nationality and main impediment to its successful adaptation to modernity. This sparked a public debate in Xining, and made 'Shokdung' a household name, provoking a range of responses from sympathy among some Amdo intellectuals to hostility among conservatives and the clergy.
13. The 'new dominion' was proclaimed upon conquest by imperial armies in 1760, comprising East Turkestan, Zungaria and the Pamir Tadjik territory in the far west. It slipped out of Qing control a century later, however, and firm rule from Beijing was re-established only in 1949–50.
14. '*Pho shul bcad de mo shul la gtugs*' is a common idiomatic phrase referring to the last stand of a people fighting to the death.

4. A LESSON IN THE PEACEFUL WAY TO RESOLVE ALL

1. This is a gentle mockery of common-place religious terminology: 'explanation and accomplishment' (*bShad sgrub*) refers to the two basic aspects of religious instruction: listening to the explanation of the teachings and putting them into practice; 'body, speech and mind' (*Lus ngag sems*) is a typical Buddhist classification of human activity; 'listening, reflection and meditation' (*Thos bsam sgom gsum*) are the three successive phases through which a student absorbs the teachings.

2. Quoted in Thomas Aquinas, *Summa Theologica*, question 95, article 2, written 1265–74.
3. Marcus Tullius Cicero, *De Legibus*, 1.44, 2.11–2.14.
4. John Locke, *Second Treatise of Civil Government*, Chapter 19, section 222.
5. Correction: it is in Sanskrit, as acknowledged below.
6. The Tibetan word for 'Buddhist' is 'insider' (*Nang pa*), as opposed to followers of the common religion, called 'outsiders' (*Phyi pa*), and it originated in pre-Islamic India, when the two religions cohabited and competed in many parts of the country. The derogatory term 'heretic', or 'holder of wrong views' (*Mu stegs pa*), is used in classical Tibetan to denote Hindu holy men of various kinds, all hostile to Buddhism. Principal doctrinal differences between the two were belief in a creator god and in an eternal soul.
7. In the Indo-Tibetan Buddhist tradition, the entirety of the Buddha's teachings are enumerated as 84,000, each intended to correct or counteract a certain deluded mental state or action.
8. The story of Shravan, who devotedly served his blind hermit parents in the forest, and was ultimately rewarded by the gods for filial piety, is known to Tibetan Buddhists through the Jataka stories of the Buddha's past lives. The Avadana-kalpalata by the eleventh-century Kashmiri poet Ksemendra has long been the canonical compilation of these stories in Tibet.
9. The story of King Drimé Kunden, the saintly prince who renounces all for the sake of virtue, also has its origins in the Indian Buddhajataka, and became the subject of a popular opera in Tibet, dramatising the agonising compassion of the Bodhisattva path.
10. This is a reference to the former theocratic Tibetan state, a system of government in which political and religious authority were unified.
11. M.N. Roy, *India in Transition*. Bombay: Nanchiketa, 1971, pp. 202–10.
12. Romain Rolland, Mahatma Gandhi: *The Man Who Became One with the Universal Being*. London: The Swarthmore Press, 1924.
13. Albert Einstein, *On Peace*. New York: Simon and Schuster, 1960.
14. Speech delivered on All-India Radio on the day of Gandhi's assassination, in the evening, 30 January 1948.

15. This phrase is used in Chinese Communist ideology to describe the 'feudal' social and political order that prevailed in Tibet before 'Liberation'.
16. A colloquial phrase in the author's native Amdo dialect, conveying clumsiness and ineptitude.
17. Disapproval of the trade in endangered wild animals expressed by the Dalai Lama during the Kalachakra empowerment at Amaravati in January 2006 led to popular demonstrations, especially in nomadic areas of eastern Tibet, at which participants set fire to robes and garments trimmed with the pelts of wild animals, signifying enthusiasm for the Buddhist ideal of non-violence and, indirectly, for the Dalai Lama. These demonstrations were initially tolerated by the authorities as non-political, but later banned. Now wearing animal furs is actively encouraged by the Chinese authorities in order to indicate a political standpoint against the Dalai Lama. See report by the International Campaign for Tibet, 23 January 2015, 'Online outrage over officials at Party meeting in Tibet wearing endangered animal furs', at: https://www.savetibet.org/online-outrage-over-officials-at-party-meeting-in-tibet-wearing-endangered-animal-furs/#sthash.Ir27u3U5.dpuf
18. Despite a state of virtual martial law following the 2008 uprising, numerous protests took place during 2009, both over local issues such as mining, and against the Chinese government's Tibet policies. The exile media reported protests in, for example, Dzogang, Markham and Jomda in TAR, Litang and Kandze in Sichuan, Machu and Labrang in Gansu. There was a widespread boycott of New Year celebrations, in protest and mourning for the suppression of the 2008 protests, especially in Ngaba and Kandze; and in Kandze prefecture especially, farmers refused to plant their fields in protest. In 2010 there was a major protest by students in Qinghai province against new laws downgrading bilingual education. All of these protests led to confrontations with the security forces and further arrests. The first self-immolation protest in Tibet took place in Ngaba in February 2009, and in 2011 these acts of protest multiplied. Over 140 have been reported at the time of writing (August 2015). The International Campaign for Tibet keeps an updated list detailing the self-immolations in Tibet and in exile, at:

http://www.savetibet.org/resources/fact-sheets/self-immolations-by-tibetans/

CONCLUSION

1. The exact source for this figure is not detailed by the author. However, it is consistent with the first major scholarly book to make a well-supported argument that non-violent resistance is more effective than armed resistance in overthrowing regimes: 'Why Civil Resistance Works: The Strategic Logic of Nonviolent Conflict' by Erica Chenoweth and Maria J. Stephan (Columbia University Press, 2011). The authors analysed 323 violent and non-violent resistance campaigns between 1900 and 2006, and found that non-violent resistance campaigns were nearly twice as likely to achieve full or partial success as their violent counterparts.
2. Khata are long white greeting scarves symbolising pure intention, traditionally made of silk, offered to sacred images, religious teachers, and to ordinary people on special occasions, such as marriage, or important meetings and partings.

APPENDICES

1. The Tibetan translation appeared in the original Tibetan version of Shokdung's book, but of course is not included in this English rendering.

INDEX

INDEX

INDEX

INDEX

INDEX

INDEX

INDEX